NIGHT RIDERS
of REELFOOT LAKE

NIGHT RIDERS
of REELFOOT LAKE

By Paul J. Vanderwood

THE UNIVERSITY OF ALABAMA PRESS

Tuscaloosa

Manufactured in the United States of America

∞

The paper on which this book is printed meets the minimum requirements of
American National Standard for Information Science–Permanence of Paper for
Printed Library Materials, ANSI Z39.48-1984.

Library of Congress Cataloging-in-Publication Data

Vanderwood, Paul J.
Night Riders of Reelfoot Lake / Paul J. Vanderwood.
    p. cm.
Includes bibliographical references and index.
Originally published: Memphis : Memphis State University Press, 1969. With new
afterword.
ISBN 0-8173-5039-X (alk. paper)
1. Reelfoot Lake Region (Tenn.)—History—20th century. 2. Reelfoot Lake
Region (Tenn.)—Social conditions—20th century. 3. Frontier and pioneer life—
Tennessee—Reelfoot Lake Region. 4. Land tenure—Social aspects—Tennessee—
Reelfoot Lake Region—History—20th century. 5. Squatters—Tennessee—
Reelfoot Lake Region—History—20th century. 6. Squatter settlements—
Tennessee—Reelfoot Lake Region—History—20th century. 7. Landowners—
Tennessee—Reelfoot Lake Region—History—20th century. 8. Violence—
Reelfoot Lake Region—History—20th century. I. Title

F443.R34V3 2003
976.8'12—dc21
2003040208

British Library Cataloguing-in-Publication Data available

PREFACE

THE STORY OF the Reelfoot Lake Night Riders has long been enveloped in a romanticism that has drained it not only of its historical accuracy but also of much of its vitality. Stripped of appended inventions, the history of the Night Riders is a classic example of the struggle of American pioneers to preserve their ways against a changing society. At Reelfoot, however, the outcome was unusual. There the pioneers were not thrust aside in their battle to defend values, but instead won the struggle, a victory which eventually profited all Tennesseans.

I do not seek to make heroes of the individuals who settled around the lake. Much about them is not admirable. They certainly were not of the same mettle as the pioneers who struggled into Texas during the first half of the last century, or others who strained to reach California and Oregon. Reelfoot's settlers possessed little of the stamina and ambition that characterized many western frontiersmen. But if the concept of "pioneers" is broadened to embrace those who created new lives for themselves in new lands because they valued their individuality more than material improvement, then Reelfoot's settlers may be included. For they too, in hardship and deprivation, carved their existence from a region of high economic potential but low initial yield, willing to forego the personal comforts and financial opportunities offered by their rapidly industrializing nation for the pleasures of a simple, dignified life marked by personal freedoms. The intrusion of capitalistic enterprise backed by legal authority turned the natives into night riders.

The specific conflict concerned private versus public control of Reelfoot Lake. Entrepreneurs seeking profit from the lake and its environs produced legal title to land adjoining and under its waters, and abruptly claimed control of the lake. The legal owners then restricted fishing on the lake, which prevented the natives from earning their accustomed livelihood. They also sought to collect rent on property where the settlers had long lived and farmed without fee or restrictions. Court decisions upheld the businessmen in their endeavors.

Unimpressed by legal finery, the pioneers (or squatters) resisted, first in court and then with whips and pump guns. Guided more by their emotions than by reason, they launched a terrorist campaign in the spring of 1908 to retain their "God-given rights." Threats, violence, and bloodshed wracked the region for half a year. Finally, the State, prompted by an outraged public, subdued the terrorism and destroyed the Night Rider movement; however, the dramatic events fastened public attention upon the controversy and initiated a sequence of legal steps that brought the lake into the public domain in 1914, an outcome that gave rise to the claim that it was the Night Riders who had "freed Reelfoot Lake for all Tennesseans."

Much of the Night Rider spirit continues to pervade the lake district. There is an ambience of impending violence. Indeed, a degree of lawlessness persists. Especially among older residents, a stranger remains suspect, if not unwelcome. But a younger generation, better educated and more mindful of business opportunities, seeks to develop the region into a national attraction. To this latter group, raised on Night Rider tales and proudly mindful of its heritage, I proposed a historical investigation of the Night Rider movement.

Many participants in the events of 1908–1909 continued to reside in the area into the 1960s although, in accordance with custom, they were reluctant to discuss the affair. The interviews needed to obtain information were successfully arranged only because two young men, thoroughly familiar with the region and its inhabitants, provided introductions that encouraged old-timers to recall the night riding era. For their aid, I owe my gratitude to Billy Hayes Hall and Dan McKinnis.

Mr. Hall operated a fish dock at Samburg and over a period of months in the fall of 1956, he and I had exceptional fortune in interviews with former Riders and their victims. Mr. McKinnis, then county court clerk, later Obion County judge, sacrificed days engaged with me in research in court records in Union City, Tennessee, and Hickman, Kentucky. Together we interviewed more than fifty individuals, all of whom had been involved in the Night Rider movement. Encouraged to tell their side of the story, all of these persons supplied hitherto unpublished information about this episode of American history.

Interviews also provided much opinion that was hostile to the Night Riders. Lake County residents, who had opposed the movement vehemently, expressed their resentment. Cleve Donaldson, who had been mayor of Tiptonville in 1908, opened his records and recollections to me. So did Hillsman Taylor, a Memphis attorney, who vigorously prosecuted the Riders as the would-be assassins of his father. Among the state militiamen ordered to arrest the Riders were Ben Capell and Ben James; they recalled the period from a soldier's viewpoint.

Finally, there were discussions with surviving relatives of principals of the affair, including Ham Patterson, son of Tennessee Governor Malcolm R. Patterson, who staked his political future on the active prosecution of the Riders, and Mrs. G. W. Haynes, widow of Judge Harris, the principal target of Night Rider hatred. Many of these persons also provided their personal papers for study.

In all, more than seventy individuals were interviewed during the last third of 1956. Other interviews were conducted in succeeding years. For instance, Fred Pinion, who had been labeled a leader of the Riders, was absent from the Reelfoot region in1956. He was interviewed when he returned there in 1962. I have attempted to cull from the interviews distortions that may have occurred. Regardless of any shortcomings of the interviews, I am indebted to all of the individuals who shared their experiences with me.

Newspapers were the second important source of my material; the files that I consulted are listed in the bibliography. Night Rider activities received front page headlines throughout the United States from October, 1908, through July, 1909, and Tennessee's dailies were especially active in explaining all facets of the episode. As no known official transcript of the Night Rider trials exists—the original disappeared from the Obion County Courthouse years ago—legal proceedings against the clansmen were traced through the detailed newspaper accounts of the trials. Because the newspapers so well depict their times in style and content, I have deliberately quoted newspapers at length in the text.

Mrs. Cleo A. Hughes and Miss Kendall J. Cram and their staffs at the Tennessee State Library and Archives rendered substantial assistance in locating various manuscript collections. My gratitude also goes to personal friends who aided me in the preparation of this study.

This book is dedicated to the late Enoch L. Mitchell, professor of history at Memphis State University, who first interested me in the topic and who offered continuing advice and moral support. A scholar of Tennessee history, chairman of his department, and active participant in community affairs, he was an inspiring mentor and warm friend.

P. J. V.

Austin, Texas
January, 1969

CONTENTS

ILLUSTRATIONS

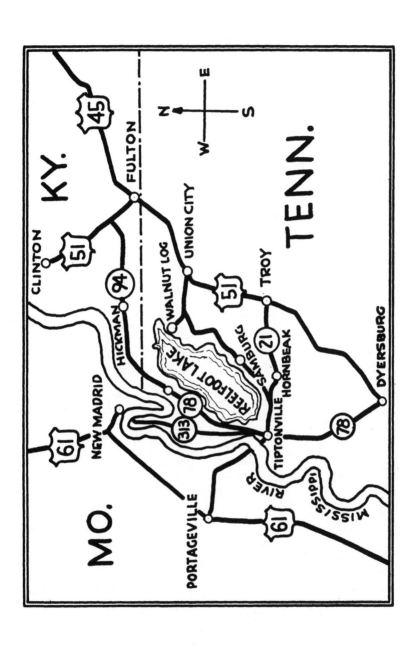

NIGHT RIDERS
of REELFOOT LAKE

CHAPTER 1

A LEGACY OF VIOLENCE

THE NIGHT RIDERS did not intend to murder Robert Z. Taylor or Quentin Rankin the night they kidnapped the two prominent Tennessee attorneys from the sportsman's lodge overlooking Reelfoot Lake. They meant only to frighten them into concessions which would allow the masked men to resume their accustomed fishing and hunting ways at the lake. This had been their goal since the outset of the night riding movement, and the unforeseen presence of the attorneys afforded the Riders a lucky opportunity to obtain the relief they sought. All they needed to do was to bend the pair to their will.

While prodding the lawyers at riflepoint through the woods toward the bayou, the Riders gruffly threatened their prisoners with execution if they refused their demands, but Taylor and Rankin did not yield. They saw no need to relent. Both were attorneys for and shareholders in the land company which controlled the lake, albeit to the detriment of their captors, who were local people once used to extracting an unmolested, if meager, livelihood from their environs. The question concerning the ownership of Reelfoot Lake had been unequivocally settled in court. The land company held full and proper title to the lake and its shores; it intended to develop them into a profitable enterprise. Desperation engendered by the judicial rulings had inclined the crude-living residents of the district toward night riding, a practice then in vogue in other parts of the South.

Irked by the obstinacy of Taylor and Rankin, the Riders produced a hangman's rope. An end was hurled over the branch of an ash tree at the edge of the bayou, and the noose fitted around Rankin's neck. Then they hoisted the lawyer. As he gagged, they demanded that he return their former fishing "rights." Lowered so that he might reply, Rankin declined to concede. The hanging process was repeated, two, three, four more times, but Rankin remained firm in will. Suddenly, a shotgun blast ripped into Rankin's body. Other shots followed, riddling the corpse. Only when the hangman released the rope did Rankin's mutilated body crumple to the ground.

Envisioning a similar fate for himself, Taylor, a vigorous sixty-year-old, bolted for freedom and plunged into the nearby bayou. The Riders, more than thirty in all, responded by blanketing the water with shotgun and rifle shot. Taylor did not reappear. Presumably, his corpse lay at the muddy bottom of the slough.

Such excesses were not uncommon to Reelfoot's Night Riders. Like many weakly disciplined, terroristic campaigns, this one had degenerated long before the Taylor-Rankin affair into a series of cruel vendettas marked by threats, whippings, house burnings, and even murder. These fearsome activities, at times conducted with the law's connivance, had gone unpunished and unpublicized, a situation that had encouraged the Riders to increasingly bolder pursuits. The assault on Taylor and Rankin was the climax, one certain to bring repercussions both feared and welcomed by the assassins. For while they feared the vengeance of man's law, they welcomed full exposure of the conditions at the lake, certain that public opinion and God's overruling justice would right the wrongs they suffered. Their work with the lawyers completed now beyond undoing, the leader of the clan admonished his men, "Burn your masks and say nothing of this night's work." [1] The night was October 21, 1908.

---

[1] *Chattanooga Daily Times,* December 22, 1908, p. 2. The assault on Taylor and Rankin is discussed in detail with complete citations in chapter III.

Unbridled violence, both human and natural, had long been indigenous to the Reelfoot region, which today comprises the northwestern corner of the state of Tennessee. The lake itself had been born of a devastating series of earthquakes in 1811–1812. Earlier the three European nations seeking hegemony in colonial North America had fought for control of the district. Even before the Europeans arrived, Indians—principally the Choctaws from what is now central Mississippi and the Chickasaws, who were natives of the sector—had competed for dominance of the abundant hunting grounds.

The French bid for supremacy failed when she lost the French and Indian War to the British in 1763; the English were eliminated twenty years later when the colonists won their independence, and the western boundary of the United States was set at the Mississippi River. For more than a decade after independence, Spain intrigued for a foothold on the eastern bank of the Mississippi, but faced by mounting pressures in Europe, she opted for United States friendship in 1795 by abandoning pretensions to territory east of the river.[2]

Soon after the American Revolution, the state of North Carolina, which then extended to the Mississippi—Tennessee did not become a state until 1796—opened its western lands for public sale. Wealthy politicians and speculators from Carolina quickly purchased the warrants which secured their title to large tracts throughout much of what was to become Tennessee, including the Reelfoot district.[3] One such speculator was George Doherty, who had been deeded 4,800 acres in Middle Tennessee in payment for his services in the Continental line.[4] Later he purchased an additional 12,000 acres in the

[2] Major sources for colonial history of the region include: Stanley John Folmsbee, Robert E. Corlew, and Enoch L. Mitchell, *History of Tennessee* (New York: Lewis Historical Publishing Company, 1960), I; Philip M. Hamer (ed.), *Tennessee, a History, 1632–1932* (New York: The American Historical Society, Inc., 1933), I; and, Samuel Cole Williams, *History of the Beginnings of West Tennessee* (Johnson City, Tenn.: Watauga Press, 1930).

[3] The complicated land question involving a triangular dispute between Tennessee, North Carolina, and the United States governments is treated in Folmsbee, Corlew, and Mitchell, *Tennessee*, I; Williams, *West Tennessee;* Thomas P. Abernethy, *From Frontier to Plantation in Tennessee* (Memphis, Tenn.: Memphis State College Press, 1955), and, Hugh Talmage Lefler and Albert Ray Newsome, *North Carolina: the History of a Southern State* (Chapel Hill, N. C.: University of North Carolina Press, [1965]).

[4] Tennessee, *North Carolina Land Grants, Charter Book A-1* (manuscript in the Tennessee State Archives), pp. 2–3.

northwest corner of the state anticipating a substantial profit from his investment as the area developed.[5] Doherty's western tracts lay in a slight depression of heavily wooded land irrigated by two streams, Reelfoot Creek and Bayou du Chien. During the earthquakes of 1811–1812 this land became the basin of a large, shallow lake, named Reelfoot after an Indian legend.[6]

The series of earthquakes that rocked the central Mississippi Valley were among the most intense the United States has ever known.[7] Beginning on December 16, 1811, the quakes shook portions of Missouri, Arkansas, Kentucky, and Tennessee for more than a year. Major destruction was confined to the natural wilderness of the area, where trees were knocked down by the thousands. New lakes appeared inland from the Mississippi, while others disappeared. On the Tennessee side of the river, the earth dome under the present-day Tiptonville rose slightly, and the wooded plain just to the east settled; as a result, the two streams, Reelfoot Creek and Bayou du Chien, overflowed and piled up against an earth dam which the quakes had built to the south. The Mississippi tore through its bank north of Tiptonville and flooded into the new basin which caused eyewitnesses to report that the river flowed backwards (north) during the upheaval.[8] The outcome was a 25,000 acre lake tucked into the northwest corner of Tennessee, with 1,000 acres spilling over

[5] Tennessee, *North Carolina Land Grants, Charter Book C* (manuscript in the Tennessee State Archives), pp. 62–63.

[6] The legend states that the prince of a Chickasaw Indian tribe inhabiting the present West Tennessee was born with a deformed foot. He walked with a rolling motion, and therefore was nicknamed Kolopin, meaning Reelfoot. When he became chief, Reelfoot sought to marry a Choctaw Indian princess, but her father would not permit it. The Great Spirit warned Reelfoot that if he attempted to kidnap the maiden, his village and people would be exterminated. Reelfoot disobeyed the Spirit. He seized the princess by force and carried her to Chickasaw territory, where Reelfoot intended to marry her. In the midst of this marriage ceremony, the Great Spirit stamped his foot in anger, causing the earth to quake. And the Father of the Waters raised the Mississippi River over its banks, inundating Reelfoot's homeland. The water flowed into an imprint left by the Spirit's foot, forming a beautiful lake beneath which Reelfoot, his bride, and people lay buried (see: Wilbur A. Nelson, "Reelfoot—an Earthquake Lake," *National Geographic Magazine*, XLV [January, 1962], 103).

[7] Myron L. Fuller, *The New Madrid Earthquake* (United States Geological Survey, Bulletin 494) (Washington, D. C.: Government Printing Office, 1912), p. 7.

[8] Walter Edgar Lowe, "History of Reelfoot Lake" (unpublished Master's

into southwestern Kentucky. Some twenty miles long and two to seven miles wide, the lake was irregular in shape and shallow enough so that stumps and trees, mainly cypress, jutted from the water. Bountiful Reelfoot Lake had been created, although it lay unexploited for the next fifty years.[9]

West of the lake lay a plain of flat land stretching to the Mississippi, much of it fertilized by periodic overflows of the river which deposited rich top soil on the terrain. This was Mississippi Valley farmland, endowed with rich agricultural qualities that soon encouraged the development of profitable plantations which knew the extremes of both social snobbery and slavery.

Different circumstances marked the east side of the lake in what became Night Rider territory. There, a high bluff, once a river bank for the wandering Mississippi and later a burial ground for the Chickasaws, rose within several hundred yards of the shore of the lake. Beyond the bluff lay rolling hills, where farming was tolerable but not overly profitable. Pioneers, ancestors of the Night Riders, established their homesteads on small farms throughout this area, although the hub of their community remained tied to settlements on the lake's shores.

The heavy forests of the Reelfoot Lake region discouraged early immigration. Trees—walnut, oak, elm, poplar, hickory, cypress, and maple—so covered the land that cultivation remained exceedingly arduous. Access might have been provided by the Obion River, but it was so full of stumps, trees, and other earthquake-caused debris that passage, even by canoe, became impractical.[10] A Carolina legislator who pioneered in the Madison and Haywood County districts of West Tennessee wrote that even though the Obion lands were "first rate," lack of good navigation reduced land values in the area.[11]

---

thesis, George Peabody College for Teachers, Nashville, 1930), p. 77. Also, L. C. Glenn, "The Geography of Reelfoot Lake," *Journal of Tennessee Academy of Science,* III (January, 1933), 3. The journal is hereinafter cited as *JTAS.*

[9] *W. E. Webster et al.* v. *James C. Harris et al.,* 3 Cates. (Tenn.), 680 (1903).

[10] E. H. Marshall (ed.), *History of Obion County* . . . (Union City, Tenn.: Daily Messenger, 1941), p. 5.

[11] Letter of Herndon Haralson, a North Carolina legislator and early settler in Davidson and Haywood Counties, quoted in Williams, *West Tennessee,* p. 153n.

As word of the natural wealth of soil and game at the lake began to circulate, interest in the region grew. Reelfoot was a prolific hatchery for black bass, pike, catfish, carp, perch, buffalo, and gar. Fur-bearing muskrat, otter, opposum, and deer were plentiful along the shores and low-lying islands in the lake. A few bear remained. Valuable timber under and around the waters belonged to those who would cut and take it, while hunters and fishermen drew upon the other natural resources at will. Gradually the country began to be settled, but with a pioneer carelessness toward land titles.[12] William Henry founded Wheeling (later Samburg) in 1852 as a lakeside landing where fish could be bought wholesale and sportsmen could find guides.[13] The newcomers believed that God had placed the bounty there for all to enjoy. That "their" land, and even the lake, might already be private property belonging to others never occurred to the settlers. This was their home, and they had come to stay.

The obvious potential for easy profit in the lake district was not lost on entrepreneurs in the region who did understand the value of legitimate land deeds and the power of the law to uphold them. It seemed to them that the person who held deeds to land under Reelfoot would control the lake itself, and therefore, the entire economy of the region. A search of land grant records revealed that a haphazard pattern of old North Carolina grants blanketed the area. Because of this crazy quilt of deeds, Tennesseans began to challenge the legality of the Carolina grants. They were abetted by the state of Tennessee which was anxious to issue new land titles in order to increase state revenues. These Tennessee deeds often overlapped the original Carolina grants, creating a legal entanglement which was not resolved until 1914, when Reelfoot Lake officially became public domain.[14]

The first Tennessee grant in the Reelfoot region went to Charles Nix in 1831. It included seventy acres north of the Doherty tracts,[15] but none of them lay beneath the lake. Reelfoot itself was considered

---

12 Don Marquis, "Menace of the Mask, pt. I; Tennessee's Tragic Story of Night Riders who Lynched at Reelfoot Lake," *Uncle Remus's, the Home Magazine,* XXIV (December, 1908), 17.

13 Marshall, *Obion,* p. 255.

14 *News-Scimitar* (Memphis, Tenn.), January 6, 1914, p. 1.

15 *Webster* v. *Harris,* 3 Cates. (Tenn.) 672 (1903).

public property until 1853, when Walter H. Caldwell procured Tennessee titles to 10,000 acres beneath the lake, some of them in conflict with the old Doherty grants. Caldwell added 5,000 acres in 1860, but he made no attempt to control the waters.[16]

In 1872, Caldwell conveyed title to his claims to a group of local men, including W. M. Wilson, who lived in the town of Obion, and Judge S. W. Cochran of nearby Troy.[17] These new titleholders considered themselves legal owners of the lake, and although they made no attempt to prevent the settlers (or squatters) from exploiting the area for pleasure or food, they began to lease the profit-making potential of the lake to entrepreneurs. John Carlos Burdick, who had recently arrived in the region from Cairo, Illinois, seeking to establish a fish business, received the wholesale fishing concession. John Ratliff paid a $100 fee for the right to draw a specified number of logs from the lake.[18]

The local people ignored the new claims to exclusive ownership of the lake. They fished and hunted as before, and, if necessary, sold part of their catch to passersby for their livelihood. Logs needed for whatever purpose were simply drawn from the lake as they always had been. Unable to check the pioneers in these encroachments and unwilling to pay royalties for products others secured at no expense, Ratliff and Burdick reneged on their lease agreements. Ratliff told Wilson that the natives were correct in their assertion that the lake was public and always had been; therefore, he would pay no further royalties for lumber.[19] The natives, in turn, supported Ratliff; they told Wilson he would be used for fish bait if he interfered with Ratliff's operation.[20] After making several twenty-five dollar payments, Burdick also terminated his lease. Wilson and the other "owners" declined to contest the issue with the local people. Wilson later said that they willingly surrendered monopolistic control of the lake

[16] *Nashville Banner,* October 22, 1908, p. 12. Also, McGill and Craig, *JTAS,* VIII, 15–16; and, Tennessee, 56th General Assembly, 1909, House, Reelfoot Lake Committee, "Report of the special committee appointed to investigate conditions at Reelfoot Lake," in *House Journal of the Fifty-Sixth General Assembly of the State of Tennessee* (Nashville, Tenn.: McQuiddy Printing Co., 1909), pp. 489–507. Hereinafter cited as *House Journal.*

[17] *Nashville Banner,* October 22, 1908, p. 12; *House Journal,* p. 493.

[18] *Nashville Banner,* March 17, 1909, p. 7.

[19] *Ibid.*

[20] *Hickman Courier* (Ky.), March 18, 1909, p. 7.

because they doubted the soundness of their title to the property; therefore, they could not press the matter in court.[21] But the animosity of the natives undoubtedly helped them to reach that decision.

Three years after these events, in 1875, William Galloway and O. H. P. Bennett of Columbia, Tennessee, discovered, or so they believed, that a legal technicality voided the Caldwell grants, and so procured for themselves new title from the state to land beneath Reelfoot.[22] This made the third set of overlapping titles—Doherty, Caldwell, and Galloway—issued for the same property. Litigation had to follow.

Bennett and Galloway leased fishing rights on "their" lake to Captain Andy Meadows of Nashville. Owners of the Caldwell property countered by seeking a chancery court restraining order against Meadows. The court upheld the validity of the Caldwell titles, giving them preference where they conflicted with those of Galloway and Bennett.[23] The Doherty grants were not at issue in this hearing; therefore, the court did not rule on their legality. As a result of the court's determination, Meadows lost his lease, and because there was no effective means of controlling any business monopoly on the lake, the waters, for practical purposes, remained public. For their part, the natives did not concern themselves with the juridical maneuvers going on around them. No legalism could alter their opinion that the lake was public, to be enjoyed by all. So they continued to hunt and fish without restraint, selling their catch to whom they pleased, and paying no one for any privileges.

While the judicial flurry passed without causing great concern or change at the lake, at least one person followed the proceedings with dedicated interest. His name was James C. Harris, a willful North Carolinian, who was quietly obsessed with an ambition to own the lake. Harris had journeyed to the region in about 1865 seeking wealth in what was designated as Lake County in 1870.[24] From the beginning he harbored plans to drain the lake for its value in lumber

21 *Ibid., Nashville Banner*, March 17, 1909, p. 7.

22 *Nashville Banner*, March 17, 1909, p. 12; *House Journal*, pp. 492–93.

23 *Nashville Banner*, October 22, 1908, p. 12; *House Journal*, p. 493.

24 Personal interview on December 17, 1956, with Mrs. G. W. Haynes, who married Judge Harris, a son of J. C. Harris, said to be a relative of Edward Harris, a deputy surveyor of West Tennessee who amassed considerable land for himself. Also, personal interview on October 20, 1956, with Cleve Donald-

and at the same time to acquire some of the Mississippi Valley's most fertile soil, ideal for lucrative cotton production. For twenty years Harris toiled to achieve the wealth he believed necessary to purchase the lake from the various title holders. He cut timber from what were at first modest land holdings and sold the wood as fuel to steamships on the nearby Mississippi. He then cultivated the cleared land in cotton, and profits from these endeavors were invested in more land. The process had been repeated for two decades, and by 1890, J. C. Harris was counted among the most prosperous landowners in the region. He then began to formalize plans for the purchase of Reelfoot Lake.[25]

Meanwhile, owners of the Caldwell title, which had been declared valid in court, were attempting to strengthen their claims to ownership of the lake by purchasing additional land in the district. They received a grant for a new tract from the state in 1897, but then unexpectedly in the same year they sold their entire holdings to the Reelfoot Outing Company, a sporting club formed by a group of men from Louisville, Kentucky.[26] The sportsmen began to develop the lake into a private resort. A clubhouse was erected on an island in the lake, and the "sports," as the natives called the visitors, began arriving for vacations and weekend relaxation. Suspicious of the wealthy visitors and aware that the outing club aimed to regulate the lake, the settlers responded with a campaign of harassment. "Sports" guided by the natives seldom experienced a decent catch and often met with exasperating "accidents." The local game warden, never before one to trouble himself over frequent violations of state and local laws by the lake people with whom he was friendly, zealously prosecuted infractions by the "sports," who were then fined by local magistrates. And the natives could get even tougher. When the outing company hired surveyors to plot the exact boundaries of its tract, the employees were run off at gunpoint and warned not to return.[27] Then when the company attempted to prevent the na-

---

son, a long-time resident and self-styled historian of the Reelfoot district. Hereinafter cited as "Haynes interview" and "Donaldson interview."

[25] Haynes interview and Donaldson interview.

[26] *House Journal*, p. 493.

[27] *Ibid.; Nashville Banner*, October 20, 1908, p. 9; and personal interview on December 15, 1956, with Joe Johnson of Midway, Tenn., a self-admitted former Night Rider. Hereinafter cited as "Johnson interview."

tives from taking lumber from the lake, a vigilante party of local people threatened reprisals.[28] Within a year the sportsmen realized they could not cope with the tactics of the natives, and on December 28, 1898, the club sold all of its property for $5,400 to J. C. Harris,[29] who had unobtrusively been pursuing his aspiration to own the lake.

Between 1895 and 1897, a series of Tennessee grants had been made to friends of Harris, apparently to mask his design, and then had been transferred to the Harris estate.[30] Realizing that the riparian rights of lakeside owners could create legal problems for his drainage project, Harris also had purchased large quantities of property along the shoreline.[31] The old Doherty tracts had been acquired, and with the culminating purchase from the outing company, Harris' land puzzle appeared to be completely and legally assembled.

In August, 1899, Harris announced ownership of the lake and said he intended to drain it by excavating a canal from the natural drainage outlet at the south end to the Mississippi River.[32] A dredgeboat was carried piecemeal from the Mississippi to the washout, where it was reassembled. More than 175 teams of mules were used to clear a path for the canal through the thick woods and dense undergrowth. The natives saw their life's work and recreation ebbing away, and they realized that Harris could not be bluffed.[33] So they pooled funds, and although skeptical of the law, hired attorneys to carry their complaint to court, where a judge might understand the urgency and legitimacy of their cause and terminate the ambitions of J. C. Harris.

Representing themselves as owners of land, hotels, docks, and other enterprises situated along the Obion shoreline, the longtime settlers, led by J. C. Burdick, asked Chancery Court Judge W. H.

---

[28] Johnson interview; *Nashville Tennessean*, October 28, 1908, p. 8.

[29] *House Journal*, p. 493.

[30] J. T. McGill and W. W. Craig, "The Ownership of Reelfoot Lake," *JTAS*, VII (January, 1933), 16.

[31] *House Journal*, pp. 493–94.

[32] *Webster* v. *Harris*, 3 Cates. (Tenn.), 672 (1903).

[33] Personal interview on November 17, 1956, with Fon J. Lasater, self-admitted former Night Rider, who lived near Blue Bayou at Reelfoot Lake. Hereinafter cited as "Lasater interview."

Swiggart in 1902 to enjoin Harris from draining the lake. While insisting that their riparian rights would be irreparably damaged by Harris' project, they also questioned the right of any individual to own Reelfoot Lake. This latter point was an important constitutional issue that concerned the navigability of the lake. If, under the law, Reelfoot was navigable, it was public domain in accordance with the state constitution. If not, it was subject to private control. Finally, the complainants insisted that draining the lake would endanger public health by exposing its bottom of decaying vegetable matter.[34] Harris argued that he held unalterable legal title to all land around and under the lake, which was too shallow and full of trees to be considered navigable, and therefore could be privately owned— and drained, if the owner so wished.

Chancellor Swiggart found for the natives and enjoined Harris from draining the lake. To drain Reelfoot would violate the rights of "certain landowners," he ruled. Even more important, however, the chancellor decided that the lake "is a public and navigable body of water in the sense of the law as well as in fact, and therefore not the subject of private ownership and control . . ." [35] Therefore, Reelfoot belonged to all Tennesseans and deeds to land beneath the water were void.[36]

Undeterred by the chancellor's decision, Harris hired three of West Tennessee's most reputable attorneys—James Deason, Quentin Rankin, and Seid Waddell—to carry an appeal to the State Supreme Court. Meeting in Jackson, Tennessee, for the April term of 1902, the high court upheld the injunction which prevented Harris from draining the lake but on grounds that Harris had not proved clear and exclusive ownership to all of the land beneath the waters. Then on the vital issue concerning private-versus-public ownership of the lake, the Supreme Court reversed Chancellor Swiggart and ruled that Reelfoot was susceptible to private ownership because it was too shallow and too full of rotting stumps to be considered navigable.[37] If an individual could prove title to all parcels beneath Reelfoot, then he had the right to control use of the lake. The deci-

---

[34] *Webster* v. *Harris*, 3 Cates. (Tenn.), 672–73 (1903).
[35] *Ibid.*, 674–75.
[36] *Ibid.*
[37] *Ibid.*, 703–04.

sion amounted to an open proposal to J. C. Harris to perfect his claim and then do as he might with the lake. Harris, of course, accepted the "invitation."

When Harris died in 1903, he bequeathed his holdings at the lake to his son, Judge (a given name) Harris. Whether Judge Harris ever intended to drain the lake is an unanswered question. His father certainly meant that he should, and within ten years, or else suffer loss of the inheritance.[38] But Judge Harris made his own decisions, and even if he did not propose to drain the lake, he did intend to own and exploit it.[39]

By 1905 the Harris estate had purchased all of the land under the lake and ninety per cent of the shoreline[40] at a total cost of $8,400.[41] As the purported owner, Judge Harris then entered chancery court and sought to enjoin all persons from using the lake without his permission. This suit was contested by John Shaw and Walter Pleasant, partners in a fish dock business at Samburg, who noted that Harris did not own the former Galloway grants, a portion of them under the lake, and therefore he could not assert control of the lake. The dock operators were represented by Deason and Rankin, two of the lawyers who had presented James Harris' case to the Supreme Court in 1902, and by Robert Z. Taylor, one of their frequent law associates who was also politically influential in Tennessee. While they certainly intended to represent their clients fairly, the attorneys also saw a way to "do business" with Harris.

The court once again frustrated Harris' ambitions. It ruled that because he did not own the Galloway land, he could not claim ownership of the lake. While the case was still in litigation, however, Rankin, Taylor, and Deason had quietly purchased the grants in question, paying $300 for the valuable land to the Galloway heirs, two elderly ladies in Columbia, Tennessee.[42] They then informed Harris that the property was not for sale—but that they looked favorably upon the

---

38 Personal interview on December 15, 1956, with W. M. Miles, a Union City attorney and close friend of J. C. Harris. Miles spoke with Harris just before Harris died. Hereinafter cited as "Miles interview."

39 Haynes interview.

40 Marquis, *Uncle Remus's, the Home Magazine*, XXIV (December, 1908), 17.

41 *House Journal*, p. 494.

42 *Ibid.;* Lowe, "History of Reelfoot Lake," pp. 149–50.

creation of a corporation in which they all would have a stock and a voice in control of Reelfoot Lake. Harris had no alternative. The West Tennessee Land Company was formally chartered on July 31, 1907, and Harris, Taylor, Waddell, Deason, and F. W. Moore were listed as incorporators.[43] The merger of these property interests confirmed private ownership of the lake. What recourse was left to the natives?

The company was capitalized at $125,000, with Harris controlling fifty-one per cent of the stock and the attorneys, along with Shaw and Pleasant, the other forty-nine per cent.[44] J. C. Burdick leased the fishing rights for nine years, paying the company a monthly royalty of one-half cent per pound for the first 60,000 pounds of fish sold by the wholesaler and one-quarter cent per pound after that. It was not unusual for Reelfoot to yield more than 100,000 pounds of fish a month,[45] and both the owners and the wholesaler envisioned a solid profit from their agreement. Although there were no restrictions against fishing and hunting for food and pleasure, the natives were compelled to transact their business through Burdick's dock, situated at Shaw's Park, just above Samburg.[46]

Burdick, a longtime friend of the fishermen and often the instigator of their opposition to the Harris interests, was criticized by the settlers for his alliance with the land company, but he had little choice in the matter. He either had to come to terms with the land company or leave Reelfoot Lake. To meet the royalty payments Burdick reduced the price given fishermen for their catch. Unwilling, and in some cases unable, to stand the loss in income, which was already marginal, some fishermen ignored Burdick's restrictions and bootlegged fish to itinerant wholesalers and others traveling the district.[47] Backed by the land company, Burdick secured court injunc-

[43] Tennessee, Department of State, "Charter Record Book Q-A" (manuscript in Tennessee State Archives, Nashville), pp. 187–88.

[44] *House Journal*, p. 494.

[45] *Nashville Banner*, March 17, 1909, p. 7.

[46] Arthur Cleveland Hall, "The Reelfoot Lake Night Riders," *The Independent*, LXVI (January, 1909), 81; *House Journal*, p. 495.

[47] Personal interview on October 20, 1956, with Bud Morris of Samburg, a former self-admitted Night Rider and sometimes leader of the organization. Hereinafter cited as "Morris interview." Also, Marquis, *Uncle Remus's, the Home Magazine*, XXIV (December, 1908), 19.

tions against those who refused to sell through his docks. Several who disobeyed such orders were fined and sent to jail in lieu of payment, while others spoke of turning to farming, at least until the monopoly was eased.[48] Nets of the fishermen rotted from lack of attention, and their families began to suffer from the financial strain. The land company further exacerbated the situation by forcing leases upon farmers who for decades had cultivated land around the lake without restrictions or concern about property rights. To the farmers, it was their land because they worked it, and so had the fathers of most of them.

The natives were bewildered. They said they thought that a compromise had been reached between themselves and Harris. In return for Harris' promise not to drain the lake and his assurance that unrestricted fishing and hunting would be allowed, the local people would not hinder Harris' efforts to develop his holdings as he desired.[49] None of this had come about. In fact, there never were any such negotiations or compromises between Harris and the natives, and talk of such only represented an attempt by the settlers to earn further sympathy for their cause. The lake people considered themselves abandoned by their educated friends and leaders. Lawyers whom they had paid to fight Harris were now officers of his land company, which sought to divest them of their property and rights. Other attorneys had been hired to pursue a court remedy but to no avail. The natives felt cheated.[50] Even former dependables like Burdick had deserted them for a profit.[51] The lower courts, bound by the Supreme Court's ruling that Reelfoot could be privately owned, and faced by a phalanx of legal deeds presented by the land company, could only secure the monopoly's position.

Chancery Court Judge John S. Cooper of Trenton on February 11, 1908, granted Judge Harris still another injunction which re-

[48] Morris interview.

[49] Marquis, *Uncle Remus's, the Home Magazine*, XXIV (December, 1908), 19; Morris interview.

[50] *St. Louis Post-Dispatch*, July 3, 1909, p. 2; Marquis, *Uncle Remus's, the Home Magazine*, XXIV (December, 1908), 19; *Hickman Courier*, October 22, 1908; p. 1; and, Morris interview.

[51] Lasater interview; Marquis, *Uncle Remus's, the Home Magazine*, XXIV (December, 1908), 18–19; and, personal interview on October 21, 1956, with Harry McQueen of the Reelfoot region, a self-admitted former Night Rider. Hereinafter cited as "McQueen interview."

strained the fishermen from seeking profit in the lake. On March 14, 1908, the natives asked Judge Cooper to dissolve this edict which they insisted prevented them from earning a livelihood. He denied the petition.[52] Baffled by legal intransigence, the natives sought a solution elsewhere, and a month later masked Night Riders inaugurated a violent campaign to "free" Reelfoot Lake.[53]

Had the settlers continued to challenge the land company's claim to exclusive control of the lake through the courts, they might have won their cause without bloodshed.[54] The company's legal position was not perfect. Conflicting claims to property around and under the lake continued. For instance, William Dickey of Temple, Texas, asserted that his great-great-grandfather, James Patterson, had been deeded 1,000 acres under Reelfoot by the state of Tennessee in 1822, and he was heir to the grant. Assuming his title to be valid, Dickey announced his intention to drain the lake.[55] This claim appears to have been spurious and nothing came of it, but others might have had more validity.

As for the Harris holdings, they were properly paid for; however, several transfers of property to him had been accomplished through quit-claim deeds by people who did not own the land themselves. This made Harris' position vulnerable. And how much property did the settlers legally hold by right of occupation?[56]

Reelfoot might have been "freed" through judicial procedure, though the process would have been long and expensive. The natives had neither the patience nor money needed for a protracted and expensive legal fight. It was a sense of immediacy born of declining income and threatened expulsion which compelled the settlers toward the kind of solution they understood best: direct, and if necessary, violent action.

[52] Marquis, *Uncle Remus's, the Home Magazine*, XXIV (December, 1908), 19; *House Journal*, pp. 495–96.

[53] Hall, *The Independent*, LXVI, 82.

[54] Marquis, *Uncle Remus's, the Home Magazine*, XXIV (December, 1908), 21.

[55] *Hickman Courier*, November 5, 1908, p. 5.

[56] Marquis, *Uncle Remus's, the Home Magazine*, XXIV (December, 1908), 21.

CHAPTER 2

THE MAKING OF NIGHT RIDERS

THE MEN DETERMINED to free Reelfoot Lake from the land company's monopoly were for the most part uneducated and unambitious, their horizons narrowly restricted to the lake and its environs.[1] Crude in dress and manner, they lived simple lives unencumbered by the pressures of a more developed society. Devoid of motivation for substantial gain, financial or other, their lives remained leisurely. Some thought them lazy.[2]

The society of the Reelfoot folk was a closed one to strangers, who were suspected of attempting to befriend, only to exploit, the settlers. Uncomfortable around others who had better manners and means, the natives preferred to be left alone. Among themselves they

[1] *Nashville Banner,* December 17, 1908, p. 4. In this detailed editorial page article the *Banner* attempts to dispel many of the romantic myths concerning the Night Riders which were created by the press and printed as supposed fact following the Rankin murder. It is one of the better background articles on the lake people.

[2] Marquis, *Uncle Remus's, the Home Magazine,* XXIV (December, 1908), 20–21.

were talkative and friendly. They had no pronounced dialect or peculiar idioms, although various communities had their own colloquialisms.[3] Around outsiders, however, the settlers tended to be silent, even morose.

There were some five hundred families around the lake who depended upon fishing for a living (although many moved away when the night riding started).[4] The majority, however, farmed corn, oats, tobacco, and cotton. Cotton yielded only half a bale per acre, for much of the soil on the Obion side of Reelfoot was a mixture of clay and stones, unlike the rich terrain that distinguished Lake County just across the lake. The natives were able to provide their own subsistence foods, such as potatoes, but the land yielded them no luxuries.[5] For most, life was unregulated, dull, and meager. The nature of the region assured them enough food and plentiful housing material plus relative seclusion. Content with such an existence, few had ever considered leaving the lake for a supposed "better life" elsewhere. All they had was their way of life—but they believed it worth fighting to protect.

Their names revealed their Anglo-Saxon stock: Ike Johnson, Frank Mitchell, John Townsley, Ed Powell, Charley Parkerson, Buck Adams, and Cap Blythe.[6] In religion they were Protestant fundamentalists, mainly Presbyterians, Methodists, and Baptists, although they seldom studied the Bible and attended church irregularly. The first sects to be represented in Obion included the Presbyterians and the Associate Reformed Presbyterians (the Seceders). Missionaries for other Protestant denominations closely followed them. The Methodist Episcopal Church South became the largest in the county, which also had some Primitive Baptists and members of the Church of Christ.[7]

Community clannishness normally limited marriage to family friends and, at times, relatives. Inbreeding further inhibited the

[3] *Nashville American*, December 17, 1908, p. 4.

[4] *House Journal*, p. 495.

[5] U. S., Bureau of the Census, *Thirteenth Census of the United States: 1910, Agriculture*, VII, 597–606.

[6] Marshall, *Obion*, p. 255.

[7] Goodspeed Publishing Company (ed.), *History of Tennessee* (Nashville: Goodspeed Publishing Company, 1887), pp. 829–31.

adoption of new lines and "progress." Social life mainly involved dances and meetings at the Odd Fellows Hall in Samburg, church gatherings, and neighborly visiting. Many spurned liquor, although bootleg whisky could be easily obtained. Hunting was a man's idea of a good day's recreation; the pump gun was his favorite weapon. Most were also proficient with rifle and pistol.[8]

The majority of the settlers were first and second generation Tennesseans with some roots in the Carolinas and Kentucky and to a lesser extent in Virginia, Georgia, and Alabama.[9] At the beginning of this century, Obion County had a population of almost 30,000, a good fifth of them around Reelfoot, the fastest growing region in the county;[10] however, Tennessee as a state lagged far behind the average national growth rate. Samburg with its general store, blacksmith shop, hotel, and 111 persons was the largest town in the lake area, although almost 2,000 persons lived in the Samburg district.[11]

The natives considered formal schooling a luxury. Parents were proud when their children could attend classes, but school, for most families, came second to work. Generally, all available hands were needed at home to help scratch out a living. The youngest children normally attended the early grades, but few advanced to high school. The lake district had twenty-eight schools, three-quarters of them offering only elementary education. All of the schools experienced low daily pupil attendance; the average eight-grade school had less than one hundred pupils, and fewer than sixty per cent of those supposed to attend school actually did so.[12] Textbooks were not uniform, and no libraries existed. Teachers earned an average of

---

[8] *Nashville American,* December 17, 1908, p. 4.

[9] U. S., Bureau of the Census, "Tenth Census (1880): Population," XXV (Tennessee: counties of Obion, Overton, and Perry), *passim* (manuscript in Tennessee State Archives, Nashville).

[10] U. S., Bureau of the Census, *Twelfth Census (1900): Population,* I; pt. 1, 373.

[11] U. S., Bureau of the Census, *Thirteenth Census (1910): Population,* III, 753. Also, *Nashville Banner,* October 23, 1908, p. 9.

[12] U. S., Bureau of the Census, *Thirteenth Census (1910),* III, 753; *The New York Times,* October 24, 1908, p. 8; and, Tennessee, Department of Education, "Annual Reports of the Obion County Superintendent of Education to State Superintendent" (manuscript in Tennessee State Archives, Nashville), years ending June 30, 1892, 1893, and 1905. Hereinafter cited as "School Reports."

$43.25 a month and manifested little interest in increasing their competence through reading circles or faculty institutes.[13] The United States Census Bureau classified twenty-five per cent of Reelfoot's population as illiterate, and the number was increasing.[14]

Whatever their social and educational shortcomings, the lake people understood the threat that the monopoly posed to their way of life. They were angered that an individual or corporation could presume private ownership of a lake in which the natives and their forefathers had fished without restrictions for half a century. They were determined that their long-held rights would not be usurped by others, whom they believed to be greedy for profit at the expense of their continuing existence at the lake. The entire situation seemed so patently unjust to the natives that they believed that they needed only to expose their plight to public scrutiny, and an aroused Tennessee citizenry would right the wrong. Thus, the Night Rider movement around Reelfoot began in part as an attempt by the natives to focus statewide attention on their problem.[15] Events occurring just to the northeast of their region provided a pattern easily adaptable to the designs of the lake people.[16]

Since 1904 the tobacco "black patch" regions of southern Kentucky and northcentral Tennessee, extending to the fringe of Obion County, had been agitated by the depredations of night riders who were attempting to regulate the tobacco business. The owners of the tobacco processing plants had banded together in a trust in order to control the price paid to tobacco farmers for their product. When the price of tobacco dropped severely, the farmers formed an association and pledged to market their tobacco to only one buyer, the highest bidder for the entire crop. Since not all of the farmers agreed to join the planters' association, the members of the group then sought to coerce the strays into line. They started with simple boycott. Association members refused to help non-members harvest their crop, gather ice, or kill hogs, those traditionally co-operative

---

13 "School Reports," *passim.*

14 U. S., Bureau of the Census, *Thirteenth Census (1910),* III, 753.

15 *House Journal,* pp. 495–96; Johnson interview and Morris interview.

16 Don Marquis, "Menace of the Mask, pt. II: Clarksdale: an Armed Camp," *Uncle Remus's, the Home Magazine,* XXIV (January, 1909), 9–10, 34–35, and 38.

efforts in farm communities. Doctors, mechanics, and merchants were asked not to trade with the recalcitrants. When the boycotts failed, the association turned to salting and scraping the tobacco beds of the hold-outs. Grass seed was tossed among their tobacco plants. These and other pressures soon progressed to night riding, arson, and whipping.[17]

Kentucky's Governor Augustus E. Willson called out the state militia to restore order, but the measure was not altogether successful.[18] Newspapers thundered against the lawlessness. Criminal trials were held, and others docketed. Although the tobacco wars had not ended, officials had been shocked into studying the situation and seeking adjustments, a lesson learned by the aggrieved people at Reelfoot Lake.[19]

Tom Johnson, his cousin Garrett, and Tom Wilson organized Reelfoot's movement.[20] Wilson and Tom Johnson were successful farmers, among the most respected in the community. Garrett Johnson had not attained the wealth or reputation of the others, but he was to prove himself ambitious, ruthless, and capable of leadership. Although strong-arm tactics were by no means unknown to Reelfoot's residents, in the spring of 1908, representatives of the lake region traveled north to consult with members of the tobacco planters' association about the intricacies of night riding. They returned with a fealty oath, password, notions concerning regalia, and suggested techniques for night riding.[21]

Small organizational meetings followed in private homes around Reelfoot Lake, and the membership began to develop. Its size fluc-

---

[17] *Ibid.*

[18] Marquis, *Uncle Remus's, the Home Magazine,* XXIV (January, 1909), 38.

[19] Marquis, *Uncle Remus's, the Home Magazine,* XXIV (December, 1908), 21; Morris interview and Johnson interview.

[20] Morris interview and Johnson interview; also, numerous newspaper references, e.g. *Chattanooga Daily Times,* December 22, 1908, p. 2; and *Nashville Tennessean,* December 23, 1908, p. 7.

[21] Morris interview. Also, personal interview on May 12, 1962, with Fred Pinion, a resident of the Reelfoot area and self-admitted former leader of the Riders; hereinafter cited as "Pinion interview." For examples of oaths, passwords, etc. of tobacco district night riders, see: *Chattanooga Daily Times,* September 19 and 23, 1908, both p. 1. These substantiate the similarities between the Tennessee and Kentucky clans.

tuated into the hundreds, but the nucleus never contained more than twenty.[22] The Riders forced some to join, such as Ed Powell, who took the oath from Garrett Johnson the night the Riders committed their most infamous crime.[23] They ordered Tid Burton to attend a meeting of the group or be hanged.[24] When William Roberts declined to join, a Night Rider leader warned him that when the gang went to Lake County to murder Judge Harris, "You'll have to go [with us] whether you want to or not." [25]

Among those who turned to night riding, only a few were fishermen. Instead the majority of the organization included hired farm hands, sharecroppers, and intermittent laborers, who saw the land they worked being surveyed for eventual seizure by the land company. Some of them had little work to do and so joined the clan. A few shrewd and successful farmers became members. They earned a comparatively good income and resented the land company's intrusions into their social and economic control of the district. In the bottomland which they controlled, there was good year-round pasturage, where they could raise mules and horses at little cost. These community elites aimed to protect their easy profits and endorsed night riding, even those who did not participate.[26]

Others who joined were mere boys seeking to escape boredom. The adventure of night riding, with its secrecy and mystery, appealed to many.[27] In fact, the entire movement lacked seriousness, not so much in purpose, as in conduct. The Riders planned and executed many of their excursions in a party atmosphere and they called themselves "Sons of Joy" and "Knights of Fun." [28] One evening they turned out the entire town of Hornbeak for a party and ordered Carlos O. Neely, a teen-ager known by the Riders because he de-

22 Hillsman Taylor, "The Night Riders of West Tennessee," *West Tennessee Historical Society Papers,* VI (1952), 78.

23 *McNairy County Independent* (Selmer, Tenn.), December 25, 1908, p. 2.

24 *Atlanta Journal,* December 28, 1908, p. 1.

25 *Atlanta Constitution,* December 26, 1908, p. 2.

26 *Nashville American,* November 23, 1908, p. 4, and December 17, 1908, p. 4. Also, personal interview on November 17, 1956, with Joe Hogg, long-time resident of the lake district and self-admitted Night Rider; hereinafter cited as "Hogg interview."

27 *Nashville American,* December 17, 1908, p. 4.

28 *News-Scimitar,* November 5, 1908, p. 1.

livered mail in the Samburg area, to conduct the Hornbeak town band in concert, "and make every other song 'Dixie'." Neely complied ("I was so scared, it was the only time in my life I was able to doublelip my cornet"), and after three hours of revelry, the Night Riders fired their guns into the air and left.[29] Hornbeak citizenry vowed to challenge the Riders with rifles rather than entertain them with instruments if they returned, and lookouts were posted nightly on rooftops to warn of any approaching masked men. But the Riders never returned. Fearful of recognition which could lead to retaliation, they seldom visited the same people or the same place twice.

A minor criminal element and local riffraff crept into the membership—men like Frank Fehringer, a petty bootlegger. Talkative and active, but with utterly no community standing, Fehringer became a leader of the Riders,[30] an indication of the looseness and pliability of the membership.

There may have been one woman in the band. Ella (sometimes Alice) Pride complained to authorities that she had been stripped and beaten by the Riders until she consented to become their secretary. Forced to wear masculine clothing, she said she accompanied the Riders on their raids under threat of death. For some time she supposedly handled correspondence with similar organizations in other states, although none of this correspondence has ever turned up. Neither have any of the organization's records which Mrs. Pride said she kept but later burned.[31] That Mrs. Pride, who was some forty years old, gloried in calling herself a Night Rider is probably closer to the truth. But the band would have none of her and finally administered her a sound whipping for her loose talk.[32] Mrs. Pride may have helped arrange meetings of the Riders, but it is doubtful that she ever rode with them. Nor did black men. Reelfoot's popu-

[29] Personal interview on November 18, 1956, with Carlos Neely.

[30] *Chattanooga Daily Times*, December 22, 1908, p. 2; Marquis, *Uncle Remus's, the Home Magazine*, XXIV (December, 1908), 21; and, Morris interview.

[31] *St. Louis Post-Dispatch*, November 5, 1908, p. 1; *News-Scimitar*, November 5, 1908, p. 1.

[32] Personal interviews on November 17, 1956, with Mrs. Guy Settle and William Tidwell, who knew Ella Pride as a friend of the Night Rider movement.

lation was almost twenty per cent black,[33] but none was permitted in the clan.[34] The Night Riders, like most whites in the district, held a crass race prejudice against the black men, few of whom had progressed much beyond slavery.

Reelfoot's organization had an oath similar to that of the Kentucky riders, basically designed to silence members about the band's activities. The leaders invoked the will of God into the simple pledge, and the penalty for relating any of the group's secrets was "death, hell and destruction," and "Your body will not be buried in a graveyard." [35] It is doubtful that the clan's leaders ever assessed the death penalty to a member for a violation of his oath. Despite such trappings, the Night Riders did not develop into a rigidly bound, highly secretive organization. If they felt any dedication, it was to their cause rather than to their clan as such. Members who strayed were coerced back into line; rarely, if ever, were they punished for their misdemeanors. State investigators first thought that John McBride had been executed near Hickman, Kentucky, for an oath violation. At least this was the information provided by his sweetheart who lamented that his body never had been found;[36] however, McBride's mother later asserted that her son was alive and working in Arkansas.[37]

The Night Riders used "seven wonders" as one of their passwords, the counter-reply being, "I wonder;" [38] however, they seldom employed these formalities. To this day self-admitted former Riders respect the sanctity of their oath and hesitate to discuss the movement. They are also reluctant to talk about their past because they do not understand that the statute of limitations protects them from possible prosecution for any crimes they may have committed. They can recall at least part of their oath, but the seldom-used passwords have been forgotten.

The Riders divided themselves into the Lower Lake and Upper Lake gangs. The Lower encompassed the Samburg region, while the

33 U. S., Bureau of the Census, *Thirteenth Census (1910)*, III, 756.

34 Morris interview.

35 *The Commercial Appeal* (Memphis, Tenn.), December 22, 1908, p. 1.

36 *Ibid.*, October 29, 1908, p. 2., and November 17, 1908, p. 1.

37 *Hickman Courier*, December 22, 1908, p. 1.

38 *The Commercial Appeal*, December 22, 1908, p. 1.

Upper covered Walnut Log and north and included the group from Clayton, Kentucky.[39] The bands usually operated independently, but for major raids they combined forces. Meeting places varied. Most of the time a few neighbors would informally decide to make a "visit" and ask friends for assistance. They seldom prearranged the raids. For large assemblies, the Riders gathered at Bogus Hollow, a protected area in the bluffs above Samburg; the Fitz Smith sawdust pile on the southside of Reelfoot Creek; or the Buck Eskew Woods, three miles from Walnut Log.[40] Leaders generally called these meetings to indoctrinate membership further with the goals of the organization. Usually the gatherings resembled pep rallies enlivened by liquor. Among the speakers appeared notables from the region, men who encouraged the movement but who could not ride with it for professional reasons. The Riders counted on these educated sympathizers to acquaint authorities with their complaints and to lead the search for a solution.[41]

When on a raid the Riders wore masks and gowns or capes. Their masks, fashioned from mealsacks or umbrella coverings and secured by strings stretched around the back of the head and under the chin, hid the wearer's face and the sides of his head. The bottoms of the masks were trimmed to a point and then fringed to approximate a beard.[42] A stripe of white paint or tape often circled the slits for one's mouth and eyes. The Riders generally designed their capes and gowns of plain calico, although some were of brightly colored, even flowered, bed quilt material. They wore a broad white stripe down each trouser leg, and on some gowns, a number was sewn in white over the left breast.[43] Others then referred to the wearer by number instead of by name, a practice intended to preserve the Rider's anonymity.[44] Ironically, the clansmen purchased most of the material they used for their uniforms at the general store of John Shaw

[39] *Nashville Tennessean,* November 12, 1908, p. 6, and December 22, 1908, p. 3.

[40] *Nashville Tennessean,* December 22, 1908, p. 1, and December 23, 1908, p. 7; *Nashville American,* November 12, 1908, p. 1.

[41] Morris interview and Pinion interview.

[42] *The Commercial Appeal,* November 15, 1908, p. 3, and December 22, 1908, p. 2.

[43] *McNairy County Independent,* December 25, 1908, p. 2.

[44] Morris interview.

in Samburg,[45] the same Shaw they detested because of his earlier co-operation with the West Tennessee Land Company.

In a sense, the entire movement was homemade. The Riders accumulated no treasury. There were no regular dues or assessments. Leaders of Reelfoot's Riders did not care to impose additional hardships on their already financially hard-pressed membership. They solicited no contributions from wealthy supporters nor extorted any from those who opposed them;[46] however, the better organized tobacco planters' association made several donations, which helped provide food for the families of particularly hard-pressed clansmen.[47] When they desired newspaper space, they either coerced the editor into providing it or found a sympathetic publisher. The Riders forced E. M. Tate to write a letter to the *Troy News-Banner* in which they listed their grievances and promised to befriend Judge Harris if he would ask the court to withdraw its restraining order against them. When extra guns and horses were needed for a raid, they "borrowed" them from the local citizenry. Many loaned willingly; others dared not refuse. But the Riders had the reputation of returning "borrowed" goods. Materials, such as coal oil needed for arson, were simply appropriated from a general store, and proprietors made no open protests.[48]

For seven months—from April to October, 1908—the Reelfoot region writhed in an atmosphere of terror and violence. Handicapped by the lack of capable leaders and therefore planned direction, the organization wandered from its primary objective: the destruction of the monopoly which the land company held over Reelfoot Lake. Instead, members used the organization to vent their personal spite upon individuals, and the movement gravitated toward an attempt to regulate the affairs, public and personal, of everyone around the lake.[49]

[45] *The Commercial Appeal*, October 31, 1908, p. 1.

[46] *Ibid.*; Johnson interview.

[47] *St. Louis Post-Dispatch*, November 5, 1908, p. 1; Pinion interview. The natives pooled money to pay attorneys to carry their cause to court before night riding began. Once the organization was founded, no dues were paid.

[48] *The Commercial Appeal*, November 28, 1908, p. 1; *Nashville Banner*, November 20, 1908, p. 14; Pinion interview and Morris interview.

[49] *Chattanooga Daily Times*, December 14, 1908, p. 1; Marquis, *Uncle Remus's, the Home Magazine*, XXIV (December, 1908), 21.

They brutally whipped Mrs. Emma Johnson with a briar bush because she sued her husband Joe, a Night Rider thirty years her senior, for divorce. The Riders finally allowed her to proceed with the divorce, even promising her child support, but they stipulated she must not demand any of her husband's property in the settlement.[50] Another woman who refused to return to her drunken husband was lashed to a tree and whipped. They ordered a third, fond of pretty clothing, to wear more modest garments.[51] A man in Troy felt the lash for departing with his wife's money, and another for placing his pool-playing ahead of his work.[52] Immoral women received whippings along with husbands and sons who refused to support their families. When Harvey Fagan declined to cut wood for his wife, she called on the Riders. First they whipped Fagan, and then they put a harness around his neck and forced him to work half the night plowing a field. Finally, they locked him in a stable with a store of corn and hay. As his tormentors departed, Fagan shouted, "Hey, boys, you forgot to curry me." The Riders returned to give Fagan "the currying of his life." [53]

Authorities who attempted to serve injunctions and warrants at the lake were relieved of their official papers and ordered away.[54] The Riders warned E. M. Brown and H. S. Sutton, land rental agents for Harris, not to represent him in any further transactions. Then the clansmen burned various contracts which the agents had drawn with local individuals on behalf of Harris.[55] When a Rider coveted another man's cottage, he forced the owner to take $100 for his investment in the home and ordered him to leave the region. In another instance, a Negro was halted on a road, shot through both arms, and run off.[56]

H. B. "Con" Young, who owned a sportsman's resort hotel on the lake in partnership with Mrs. Eda Page, wanted to purchase his partner's share. She didn't care to sell and called in sympathetic

[50] *Chattanooga Daily Times,* December 22, 1908, p. 1; Johnson interview.
[51] *Chattanooga Daily Times,* December 14, 1908, p. 7.
[52] *Nashville Tennessean,* December 24, 1908, p. 7.
[53] Johnson interview.
[54] *Nashville Tennessean,* December 24, 1908, p. 7.
[55] *The Sun* (New York), December 23, 1908, p. 2.
[56] *News-Scimitar,* October 20, 1908, p. 1.

Night Riders. The clansmen gave Young ten licks with a rope and demanded that he abandon his business under pain of death.[57] He left.

Sixteen Riders told Mrs. Anna Jackson to get rid of her dogs because "peace" was needed in Bogus Hollow. Then they whipped her father and sister in her presence "because they talked too much." Mrs. Jackson's orphan daughter was accused of quarreling with a neighbor's daughter, and they warned the mother to "get it stopped." Finally, the intruders gave her father three days to leave the territory, and when he did, they burned his house. Because her father complained to authorities about the arson, the Riders again visited Mrs. Jackson, brandishing a rope and vowing to hang her father. Under such pressure, Mrs. Jackson moved to Tiptonville in Lake County.[58]

Beyond the few who boasted of being Riders, one could not be certain about the membership of the band. Loose talk concerning individuals might be construed as criticism of the Riders and earn the gossiper a whipping. Neighbors suspected one another but said nothing.[59] This atmosphere—nourished by complacent local law enforcement—permitted the Riders to continue their rampage without fear of consequence.

Emboldened by their early successes, the Riders became more flagrant in their depredations. They threatened to attack and destroy Union City, the Obion County seat, where a more sophisticated populace brooked no tolerance of night riding violence. While there, they planned to whip Circuit Court Judge Joseph E. Jones, Seid Waddell (an officer in the land company), District Attorney D. J. Caldwell—even Caldwell's eighty-year-old-father—and anyone else striving to enforce the law against them. The men of Union City carried sidearms by day and manned housetops at night, prepared to resist the predicted onslaught of the Reelfoot band.[60]

57 Marquis, *Uncle Remus's, the Home Magazine,* XXIV (December, 1908), 20.

58 *The Sun,* December 23, 1908, p. 2.

59 Personal interview on October 21, 1956, with Ange Shaw of Samburg. He is the stepson of John Shaw and was in Samburg during the Night Riding era. Hereinafter cited as "Shaw interview." Also personal interview with Mrs. Guy Settle.

60 *New Orleans Times-Picayune,* December 25, 1908, p. 1; Miles interview; and *The Commercial Appeal,* October 22, 1908, p. 11.

As the culmination of their campaign, the Riders intended to thrash, or perhaps slay, Judge Harris, the focal point of their hatred toward the West Tennessee Land Company. Harris proved to be a formidable opponent; he could shoot a rifle and ride a horse as well as any Rider. His life threatened many times, Harris had moved his family to Nashville and then had openly challenged the Night Riders from his Lake County redoubt. Harris fortified his Tiptonville mansion like a feudal castle under siege. No lights burned at night, and the yard was mined with explosives. By throwing a switch, Harris could have wiped out an attacking force.[61]

As inevitably occurs when a vigilante force is running unchecked, authorities and others blamed the Riders for crimes of which the clansmen had no knowledge. "Night Riders" implied free license for anyone to do as he wished around the lake. In one such instance, C. L. Walker, manager of the Mengel Box Company in Hickman, received a letter allegedly signed by Night Riders who threatened to burn down his plant. When the legitimate Riders learned of this, they immediately wrote Walker that they never had made such a threat. They even praised Walker for his reputation of giving needed employment to low-income residents of the district. This rebuttal by the Riders led the *Hickman Courier* to conclude that the original threatening note had been sent by a disgruntled local citizen.[62]

The influence of the Riders was pervasive. Masked children played Night Riders-and-lawmen instead of cowboys-and-Indians, and the lawmen generally emerged second best. Several boys in their early teens donned masks and infiltrated a Rider gathering; however, their nervousness betrayed them, and they received a whipping for their curiosity. Misbehaving youngsters were warned the Riders would "get" them, and newspapers advertised "Night Riders wear Headlight [brand] overalls." [63]

Only a minority of the populace at Reelfoot participated in the activities of the Night Riders, yet almost everyone sympathized with their objective to "free" the lake. Many had important stakes in the outcome of the conflict. Fear undoubtedly engendered some of the

[61] *The Commercial Appeal,* October 21, 1908, p. 2; Marquis, *Uncle Remus's, the Home Magazine,* XXIV (December, 1908), 17; *Nashville Tennessean,* December 25, 1908, p. 1; *Nashville Banner,* October 20, 1908, p. 9.

[62] *Hickman Courier,* October 22, 1908, p. 4.

[63] *Ibid.,* October 29, 1908, p. 9.

support,[64] but most of the citizens, while not condoning the crimes of the Riders, believed the fishermen and farmers were being wronged by the land company and the law which it upheld.[65] They believed that the anger of the Riders was justified, and reasoned that they had organized only after the courts and powerful former friends had turned against them. Now that a new solution to the local problems was being sought, the citizens felt morally obligated to their community to support the movement. Prominent persons encouraged the Riders and told them they were right in attempting to "free" Reelfoot; therefore, the initial activities of the band were not considered criminal acts, but were regarded as disobedience warranted in order to correct an intolerable situation.[66]

Some claimed that the Night Riders proposed to dominate the domestic and economic life of the community, and, if necessary, usurp the functions of the legislature and courts by establishing their own regional government.[67] State investigators later did uncover a document purported to be the constitution of the Night Riders. This "constitution" provided that banks restrict their interest charges to six per cent, merchants limit their profits to ten per cent, prices and wages be fixed, farmers expel black tenants, landlords accept crops in lieu of cash for rent, and land ownership be limited to 500 acres a person.[68]

It seems unlikely, however, that the Riders ever intended to establish their own government. They were neither administrators nor innovators. Few, if any, could even write a legible letter.[69] Their environment attuned them to administering whippings and making threats but not to setting interest rates or regulating prices and the size of farms. They aimed their coercion at individuals rather than at an entire class or race. The Riders did not appreciate blacks, but only "bad niggers" were punished. Other blacks continued to

---

[64] Taylor, *West Tennessee Historical Society Papers,* VI, 78.

[65] Hall, *The Independent,* LXVI, 79.

[66] *Ibid.* Also, personal interview on November 16, 1956, with Seymour Osborne, resident of the Reelfoot region who claims to have known most of the Riders. Hereinafter cited as "Osborne interview."

[67] Taylor, *West Tennessee Historical Society Papers,* VI, 77.

[68] *News-Scimitar,* October 29, 1908, p. 1; Hall, *The Independent,* LXVI, 83; and *Nashville Banner,* May 6, 1908, p. 12.

[69] *Nashville American,* December 17, 1908, p. 4.

work their land under the same white man's pressures that had existed long before night riding. Blacks who "understood their place" in society were safe.[70] Although the Riders had reason to scorn John Shaw, they did not try to regulate prices or profits in his general store.[71]

The Riders themselves understood the implications of their campaign. Masked night riding was punishable by death. They also regretted their inability to control their own movement;[72] however, they relied on what they considered to be the justness of their cause for protection against avenging law. Tom Johnson, an imposing leader at 6'3", 185 pounds, and distinguished by a moustache and black beard, stated their case:

> It's like this heah, stranger. God, he put them red hills up theah. An' He put some of us po' folks that He didn't have room foh no wheah else, up theah, too. An' then He saw that we couldn't make a livin' farmin', so He ordered an earthquake an' the earthquake left a big hole. Next He filled the hole with watah an' put fish in it. Then He knew we could make a livin' between farmin' and fishin'. But along comes these rich men who don't have to make no livin', and they tell us that we must not fish in the lake any mo', 'cause they owns the lake an' the fish God put theah foh us. It jus' naturally ain't right, stranger, it ain't no justice.[73]

West Tennesseans, including some at the lake, occasionally questioned how the Rider movement would end. Several demanded its demise, as did Dr. G. C. Thomas, editor of the *Lake County News* at Tiptonville, who editorialized that the Riders must "be run to the earth." Riders whom he could identify were accused by name in print. Of course, the clansmen threatened the editor:

> Sir: This is to inform you that your presence is not desired in Tennessee, and if you do not leave the state by January 1, 1909, you will be a very bad looking corpse.
>
> [Signed] Night Riders.[74]

[70] Personal interview on December 2, 1956, with Will Woodring, a Negro farmer who lived near Reelfoot Lake during the Night Rider activities.

[71] Shaw interview.

[72] Johnson interview; Morris interview; and Pinion interview.

[73] "A Dramatic Trial of Night Riders," *Current Literature*, XLVI (February, 1909), 126.

[74] Don Marquis, "Menace of the Mask, pt. IV: Sentencing of Night Riders at Union City. Personalities of the Reelfoot Region," *Uncle Remus's, the Home Magazine*, XXV (March, 1909), 20–21.

As the Riders literally whipped the region into line, they created enemies, but fear of retaliation generally kept their opposition silent. When they finally committed murder, both the membership and community support dwindled.[75] The disaffected believed the movement had exceeded reasonable bounds, and many felt genuine relief when the organization at last collapsed under the relentless pressure of an irate state.[76] But before the end came, the Riders had cut a swath of crime and misery across the territory.

[75] Hall, *The Independent,* LXVI, 79.
[76] *Atlanta Constitution,* December 25, 1908, p. 2; *Chattanooga Daily Times,* December 23, 1908, p. 1; Miles interview; and Pinion interview.

CHAPTER 3

ARSON, WHIPS, AND LYNCHING

DURING THE SEVEN months in which they wantonly bullied the Reelfoot region into submission and reigned over it without compromise, the Night Riders committed four crimes from which they gained particular notoriety. They burned the fishing docks of J. C. Burdick at Samburg, mercilessly whipped a physically handicapped Lake County official, murdered one-half of a family of Negroes outside Hickman, and finally kidnapped two of Tennessee's best-known and respected lawyers.

In their campaign against the land company, no target was more obvious to the Riders than the docks of John Burdick. They symbolized the monopoly which the Riders were determined to break, and situated at the center of Rider territory, they were highly vulnerable. Burdick controlled the largest wholesale fish business in the district.[1] Even though gross business at the lake amounted to a sub-

---

[1] Marquis, *Uncle Remus's, the Home Magazine,* XXIV (December, 1908), 17.

stantial $50,000 a year,[2] the local fishermen realized few of the proceeds. Because he had to pay the land company an annual fee to operate the business, Burdick had reduced payments to fishermen for their catch. This meant the fishermen indirectly paid the royalties, a situation which was intolerable for the natives who found their incomes dwindling to the point of severe hardship.[3]

Burdick himself managed his wholesale outlet in Union City, while two agents ran his docks: Walter Pleasant and John Shaw, the latter also proprietor of Samburg's general store. Burdick's son, Fred, generally hauled the fish from Samburg to Union City. All of these men had been active on behalf of the fishermen in earlier court struggles against the late J. C. Harris, particularly when Harris proposed to drain the lake. Now they co-operated with the Harris interests, and the natives resented this change of allegiance.

In March, 1908, the fishermen asked Chancellor John S. Cooper of Trenton to remove the injunctions which restricted their use of the lake. Judge Cooper refused, and three weeks later, in early April, officers of the land company, together with Judge Cooper, Burdick, Shaw, and Pleasant all received anonymous letters threatening their lives.[4] Burdick was warned:

Office of Justice—by order of Post: You close up that fish buis. [sic.] never to be opened again under penalty of death, Hell and the Grave. If you think this is a joke, try it for a few days longer and see.

Yours for who shall live the longest.
[Signed] NIGHT RIDER

Being in Hell, you may raise your eyes if you don't obey.[5]

Unintimidated by the threat, Burdick shoved his thumbs beneath his suspender straps and boastfully exclaimed, loudly enough for those nearby to hear, "Who do these guys think they are? Don't they know yet who runs the lake?" That insult ignited the Night Rider movement.[6]

---

[2] *Ibid.*

[3] Morris interview and Pinion interview.

[4] Marquis, *Uncle Remus's, the Home Magazine,* XXIV (December, 1908), 19.

[5] *Ibid.;* Hall, *The Independent,* LXVI, 79.

[6] Morris interview.

During the evening of April 11 some fifty fishermen, farmers, youngsters and ne'er-do-wells gathered at the Odd Fellows Hall in Samburg determined to punish the arrogant Burdick. Masked and armed, they took Shaw and several cans of gasoline from his general store. Then they marched their prisoner along with Bose Hutchcraft, a friend of Shaw's, to the docks. Fred Burdick had been warned of an impending ruckus and had gathered an armed force to repel the trouble-makers. Using Shaw as a shield, the Riders advanced. Unable to fire without hitting Shaw, Burdick's men yielded and withdrew to the taunts of the jubilant terrorists. The Riders then doused the docks with kerosene and set them afire. As the structures toppled into the lake, rebel war whoops and the crack of rifle shots resounded through the night.[7] Employees of Burdick who lived in two homes near the docks were warned to leave the district or have their dwellings burned. The employees left, but five days later their homes were burned anyway.[8] The Burdicks, who suffered a $3,000 property loss, abandoned their Reelfoot operation for the safety of Union City. Pleasant fled to Mobile, Alabama, but Shaw, with the Riders' consent, continued to manage his general store.[9]

Public and official reaction to the brazen act of arson was apathetic. Several newspapers printed short accounts of the burning but did little to interpret its causes. The sheriff of Obion County, T. J. Easterwood, did nothing.[10] William A. Mayo, a deputy sheriff in the Reelfoot region, became a member of the Riders,[11] and the county grand jury made some cautious investigatory probes.[12] Meanwhile, the Night Riders were building membership and planning future forays. One Rider, Wad Morris, alias Mollie Pitcher, memorialized the dock burning in verse:

[7] Johnson interview; Marquis, *Uncle Remus's, the Home Magazine,* XXIV (December, 1908), 19.

[8] Marquis, *Uncle Remus's, the Home Magazine,* XXIV (December, 1908), 19.

[9] Morris interview.

[10] Personal interview on December 3, 1956, with former Sheriff Easterwood at his Union City home. Hereinafter cited as "Easterwood interview."

[11] *Atlanta Constitution,* December 24, 1908, p. 1.

[12] *Nashville Tennessean,* December 22, 1908, p. 3, and December 23, 1908, p. 7; *Atlanta Journal,* December 23, 1908, p. 2.

The Odd Fellows met at Samburg hall
One bright moonlight night;
And on Shaw's way returning home
He met an awful fright.

A big masked man walked to his face
And taking him by the hand,
Says, "Come on, Shaw, and go with us,
We want you to carry the can."

Shaw walked on as quiet as you please,
Not a word did he reply;
He thought that he was all alone,
But Bose stood by his side.

They marched him off down to the park,
Where Walter Pleasant dwelled;
Shaw was thinking all the time,
"I bet they give us hell."

He walked up and gave a rap
Then leant back 'gin a post;
Says, "Get up, Walter, please don't shoot,
It's me and poor old Bose."

They say the camp had seven guns,
And they was loaded for bear;
When the Riders came and went
There wasn't any guns left there.

They had one borrowed from a neighbor friend,
Will Mayo was name;
In taking these guns they found that one
And taken it just the same.

Hubbard Huffman heard the guns,
Also saw the fire;
His mother begged him to stay with her
And go to the park tomor[row].

Hub is a man carries out his plans,
  He had been there before;
  He had taken his gun in his right hand
    And started for the door.

He jumped out and fired a shot,
  He did it for alarm;
  He hadn't travelled very far
    Till they taken him by the arm.

They robbed him of a thirty two,
  And put him in the ranks;
  Hub came back home, was very sad,
    With pockets very blank.[13]

That the Riders could with little provocation be brutal was confirmed before April passed. Later in the month a band of a dozen masked men crossed into neighboring Lake County to administer a "lesson" to a county squire, George W. Wynne, who had stated openly that Negroes were better than Night Riders. For that remark the Riders bent the aged, hunchbacked farmer bareback over a stump and mercilessly whipped him with a thorn bush. Compelled to witness the torture, his sons stood by helplessly. Ten months later Squire Wynne died without ever fully recovering from the beating.[14]

Relations between the residents of Tiptonville in Lake County and the settlers on the Obion side of Reelfoot Lake had never been good. The people of Lake County considered themselves better educated and more genteel than the "riffraff across the lake." [15] They were also protective of Judge Harris, a highly respected member of their community, whom they believed to be unduly harassed by the coarse fishermen and their friends who refused to obey the law and claimed rights they did not possess. The skepticism that Obion's lakeside

[13] *News-Scimitar,* November 12, 1908, p. 1.

[14] *Nashville American,* December 17, 1908, p. 4; personal interview on October 21, 1956, with Mrs. Truma Smith of Tiptonville, daughter of Squire Wynne.

[15] Personal interviews on October 21, 1956, with John W. Hall, Lake County constable at the time of night riding, and Cleve Donaldson, then mayor of Tiptonville.

residents felt toward the wealthy and refined reinforced their cool-
ness toward Lake County people. These attitudes created a constant tension between the two socially distinct communities; the
whipping of Squire Wynne propelled them toward open conflict.[16]
Each side anticipated an armed invasion from the other: the Night
Riders of Obion to capture and punish Judge Harris, and the Lake
County posse to avenge the Squire. The city of Tiptonville offered a
$1,000 reward, and private citizens another $1,000, for the arrest
and conviction of Squire Wynne's assailants. A fire insurance company, fearful that night riding would spread to arson in Lake County, added another $500 to the reward money. One Night Rider, Will
Watson, was quickly indicted for the thrashing of Squire Wynne and
released under $5,000 bond. Later events implicated Watson in
more flagrant offenses, and he never stood trial in Tiptonville.[17]

The main link between the counties lay at Three Bridges at the
south end of the lake, where a series of rough, wooden structures
crossed a swamp caused by overflow from the lake. Sentries from
each county were posted on their respective sides of the bridge to
spread the warning in case of intrusion by unwanted neighbors, and
more than once, blasts of the whistle on top of Tiptonville's munici-
pal water tower summoned men from their sleep to the rooftops of
their homes, armed to repulse an anticipated attack by the Night
Riders.[18] Conversely, reports that a Lake County posse was approaching would send Obion's defenders into the ditches and cotton
fields which bordered the lone road from Lake County.[19]

These were stern, self-protective measures, but law enforcement
appeared to be paralyzed in the face of the ravages of the Riders.
Sheriff Easterwood knew of the anarchy in the lake district, but he
refused to respond, saying that no official complaints that named
alleged criminals had been filed with him.[20] How could he act, if he
did not know whom to arrest? Few victims of the Riders would have
dared name their assailants, and the sheriff knew this. The clansmen

[16] *Ibid.*

[17] *News-Scimitar,* October 23, 1908, p. 1.

[18] *New Orleans Times-Picayune,* December 22, 1908, p. 11; *Nashville
Banner,* October 23, 1908, p. 8.

[19] *Nashville Tennessean,* December 22, 1908; p. 1; Shaw interview and
McQueen interview.

[20] Easterwood interview.

were specialists in punishing people for "loose talk." The truth is
that Easterwood knew most of the Riders and probably sympathized
with their goals. At least, he did not interrupt their activities unless
forced to do so by higher authorities. At this time, no such pressure
existed.

Tennessee's Governor Malcolm R. Patterson was also apprised
of the situation. Prominent citizens of Lake County wrote the governor on August 10 that their county was being terrorized by Obion's
Riders, who threatened to murder "certain individuals," burn the
county seat, and intimidate Negro laborers into leaving during the
height of cotton picking season. Lake County citizens, according to
the petition, were constantly under arms, but could not work and
perform patrol duties at the same time. Therefore, they asked for
authorities to appoint a thirty-man posse, at state expense, to patrol
the border between Lake and Obion Counties.[21]

In a telegram to the governor, Circuit Court Judge Joseph E. Jones
endorsed the sentiments expressed by the citizens in their petition,[22]
but Patterson chose not to authorize the posse. He was campaigning
for re-election, and it would have been an unwise time for him to in-
terfere in a conflict between two counties, each of whose support he
needed in the November election. Furthermore, the Obion County
Grand Jury was investigating a series of crimes committed by the
Riders, and the governor may have surmised that justice would be
rendered in due course and the movement destroyed. He did, however, appoint several lawyers to examine in general the property situation at Reelfoot Lake, with an eye toward making the lake a public
preserve.[23] That was a politically safe move.

Governor Patterson was not the only one who suspected that
private ownership of the lake did not serve the best interests of the
state. Legislators from Lake and Obion Counties, aware of the continuing conflict between the fishermen and land company, had been
lobbying in the state capital to have the lake declared public domain.[24] At the same time, attorneys for the land company were

[21] "Special Subject: Night Riders in Lake County, Tenn.—1908," in Malcolm R. Patterson Papers (Tennessee State Archives, Nashville), Box 1,
File 10.

[22] *Ibid.*

[23] *Nashville Banner,* January 7, 1909, p. 6.

[24] *Ibid.*

preparing legislation aimed at tightening its private monopoly of the lake.[25] Their primary concern at present was to earn a substantial profit while controlling the lake. If a buyer came along later and offered the right price, sale could be considered.

While the land company hoped to increase its earnings by further securing its monopoly, the Riders roamed roughshod over the Obion countryside trying to break it. John Shaw, enroute to Union City to testify before the grand jury about the dock burning, was halted by masked men, soundly whipped, and ordered back to Samburg. Shaw never did testify in that case.[26] Garrett Johnson, in the presence of other Riders, asked Mrs. Jackson if she had given the jury information about the expulsion of her father from the district and the burning of his home. She said that she had not, to which Johnson retorted, "If you were a man, I'd blow your brains out. We will hang you if you talk." [27] Johnson later told a gathering of 300 Riders at Big Woods that anyone who intended to testify before the jury must be stopped even if they had to be hanged.[28]

In early October the Riders rode north to Brownsville, just across the Kentucky state line, to teach a good lesson to Dave Walker, whom they considered to be an arrogant black farmer. Riders from the Hickman district had reported to their cohorts that Walker had insulted a white woman and had pulled a gun on a white man. These acts warranted a vengeful whipping, and the Reelfoot gang was anxious to wield the lash. When some fifty Riders approached the Walker cabin, they came with cowbells ringing at the necks of their mounts. Residents of the area believed that a horseman or two were driving cattle out of the bottoms to pasture. No one paid the intruders any attention.

The Riders found the defiant black man barricaded with his family inside his home. If the Riders wanted Dave Walker, they were going to have to pull him out, but the hooded men who approached the house were driven back by rifle fire. No one, let alone a "nigger," had ever before dared to challenge the Riders in this manner. Still,

[25] *Nashville Banner,* October 20, 1908, p. 9.

[26] *Chattanooga Daily Times,* December 23, 1908, p. 2.

[27] *Atlanta Journal,* December 23, 1908, p. 2.

[28] *Nashville Tennessean,* December 22, 1908, p. 3, and December 23, 1908, p. 7.

they expected Walker to surrender after brief resistance. When he did not do so, several clansmen crept forward and shoved kerosene-soaked rags under the cabin door and lit them. As the Walkers fled to escape incineration, the Riders deliberately murdered them. Dave Walker was first, killed on his doorstep. His twelve-year-old daughter followed and fell dead a few paces from the house. Mrs. Walker, clutching her baby at her breast, then ran into the relentless rifle fire. The baby died instantly, still cuddled by his mother as she fell mortally wounded. Three other children who struggled from the house as it collapsed were wounded by the Riders and left to die. Somehow they survived to relate the horror of their ordeal. The dead and dying Walkers lay unattended outside the remains of their home all the following day; doctors and neighbors shied away from the scene of the slaughter fearing the Riders might return.[29]

The *Louisville Herald* commented on the affair: "David Walker was an insolent and bad negro [sic.] and had done many things that were disliked by the people of the neighborhood." The paper concluded: "No excitement prevails here. No arrests have been made, and none are expected."[30] To some it was just another "nigger lynchin' " in Kentucky.

But other Kentuckians were far from complacent about the Walker massacre. "Not in the bloodiest days of border warfare between the aborigines and the white settlers was a more ghastly outrage committed . . .," railed the Louisville *Courier-Journal* in demanding that the murderers be brought to justice.[31] Kentucky's Governor Willson ordered a company of the state militia to Hickman to prevent further violence;[32] however, there was no determined investigation of the crime. Again the Night Riders had struck with impunity.

Yet there were some consequences. The Night Riders themselves were nauseated by the wanton murder of the Walkers. They had not intended to go that far with the blacks, and some of the members

[29] *Louisville Herald*, October 5, 1908, p. 1, and October 6, 1908, p. 9; *Courier-Journal* (Louisville), October 5, 1908, p. 1; personal interview on November 17, 1956, with Will Woodring, brother of Mrs. Walker; and Morris interview.

[30] *Louisville Herald*, October 6, 1908, p. 6.

[31] *Courier-Journal*, October 6, 1908, p. 6.

[32] *Ibid.*, October 9, 1908, p. 1.

of the group began to question the future of the clan.[33] External support for the movement also started to wane, a serious threat to an organization which nourished itself on local sympathy and sought widespread public approval. But these reservations were by no means fatal to the Riders and their cause. Murder was one thing, but the killing of arrogant blacks was something less.

Chancellor Cooper, on October 14, 1908, confirmed title of the land company to exclusive ownership of the lake, and perpetually prohibited the fishermen, or anyone else, from profiting on the lake without the permission of the company. This was the first of the legal decrees which explicitly designated the lake as private property,[34] and its effect revitalized the Night Riders organization and rekindled its determination to attack the core of its complaint—the West Tennessee Land Company and its monopoly. Events were already in progress which, five days after Judge Cooper's edict, would permit the Night Riders to realize this determination—events which would lead to their own demise as well as to the eventual achievement of their goal to "free" Reelfoot Lake.

Because the conflict over fishing rights had reduced its anticipated royalties from fish sales, the corporation sought other sources of income and was receptive when Fred Carpenter, a Union City lawyer, asked to lease company land on Grassy Island and Caney Ridge at the lake for timber and grazing lands.[35] Carpenter once had owned the two strips of land but had sold them when the land company was assembling its monopoly; therefore, he was knowledgeable and at ease as he negotiated the lease with Seid Waddell on a Union City street corner the afternoon of October 17. Waddell, a land company officer and also an attorney from Union City, agreed that he and two of the company's officers, Robert Z. Taylor and Quentin Rankin, would meet with Carpenter at Walnut Log on October 19 to complete the agreement. Carpenter seemed pleased; he already knew Taylor and Rankin, both personally and by reputation.[36]

[33] Pinion interview.

[34] Marquis, *Uncle Remus's, the Home Magazine,* XXIV (December, 1908), 19.

[35] *McNairy County Independent,* December 25, 1908, p. 2.

[36] *Ibid.;* Miles interview.

While discussing the possibilities of the lease, Carpenter and Waddell paid no attention to the nondescript man who stood nearby eavesdropping on their conversation. He was Arthur Cloar, a Night Rider, who hurried to the lake region to inform his companions of the impending arrival of two of the land company's highest ranking and most respected officials.[37] Leaders of the clan recognized the not-to-be-missed opportunity to wring concessions from two men who possessed the authority to grant immediate relief; there would be Night Riders at Walnut Log to meet with Rankin and Taylor.

Robert Z. Taylor was a distinguished Tennessean, still called "Colonel Taylor" by friends in recognition of his service as a teen-aged Confederate soldier during the Civil War. Robust at sixty-three, he practiced law in Trenton and was a vigorous leader of the Democratic Party in West Tennessee.[38] He was a close friend and frequent legal associate of Quentin Rankin, who at thirty-nine was considered one of the state's most promising lawyers. A graduate of Vanderbilt University, he had earned the title of "captain" by raising a company of Tennessee volunteers for service in the Spanish-American War, although the troop never saw action.[39]

Taylor and Rankin had known both sides of the Reelfoot controversy. The natives had retained them for $800 to fight the Harris interests in court, a battle which the lawyers had lost just prior to formation of the land company in 1907.[40] Then, as the corporation's lawyers, Rankin and Taylor had been paid in stock for their legal work in reinforcing the monopoly to the detriment of the local citizens.[41]

Land company officials had shied away from Night Rider territory since the outbreak of the movement in April, 1908. Their lives had been threatened on numerous occasions, and it was generally considered that the Riders would make good their threats if they ever caught a company officer in their lair. When Captain H. A.

[37] *McNairy County Independent,* December 25, 1908, p. 2.

[38] Personal interview on November 14, 1956, with Hillsman Taylor of Memphis, son of R. Z. Taylor. Hereinafter cited as "Taylor interview." Also, *The World* (New York), December 20, 1908, p. 4.

[39] *Chattanooga Daily Times,* October 23, 1908, pp. 1–2.

[40] *Hickman Courier,* October 22, 1908, p. 1.

[41] *Nashville Banner,* October 20, 1908, p. 9; *New York Herald,* October 29, 1908, p. 5.

Taylor, who held large landholdings near Hickman and was not unfriendly toward the Riders, learned that Rankin, Taylor, and Waddell intended to visit Walnut Log, a stronghold of Night Riders, he advised the lawyers against the trip.[42] Mrs. Waddell became hysterical when she learned of her husband's intentions; so Waddell canceled his plans. The Trenton attorneys, however, believed that in recent weeks the tension had eased at the lake; they also considered past threats of the Riders as little more than bluffs. Therefore, they intended to keep their appointment with Carpenter.[43]

Arriving at Walnut Log by horse-drawn hack from Hickman, the lawyers accompanied Carpenter on the afternoon of December 19 to survey the tracts he wished to lease. At dusk the three men returned to P. C. Ward's hotel, a well-known sportsman's lodge at Walnut Log, where they dined and briefly planned the next day's work. Carpenter, who was staying nearby at his sister's home, departed. The attorneys, wearied by a long day of physical exertion, went to bed shortly after nine o'clock.[44]

Meanwhile, the Night Riders were assembling. Frank Fehringer had borrowed one of Garrett Johnson's horses and had spent the day rallying the clan for what was intended to be a showdown with the land company.[45] By eleven o'clock a band of some thirty-five hooded men was ready to ride with Garrett Johnson in command. They were armed with revolvers and pump guns, and several were drinking homemade whisky.[46] One lieutenant, Bud Morris, wore a gown with the number "4" outlined in white tape on his breast. A long rope was looped around his shoulders.[47] The Riders planned to threaten Rankin and Taylor with hanging in order to coerce them into promising relief from the corporation's monopoly. If necessary, the lawyers would be whipped and forced to walk the fourteen miles to Hickman for assistance.[48]

[42] *New York Herald,* October 29, 1908, p. 5.

[43] *New Orleans Times-Picayune,* October 21, 1908, p. 1.

[44] *The Commercial Appeal,* December 20, 1908, pp. 1–2.

[45] *New Orleans Times-Picayune,* December 22, 1908, p. 11.

[46] *Chattanooga Daily Times,* December 19, 1908, p. 1; Morris interview and Pinion interview.

[47] *McNairy County Independent,* December 25, 1908, p. 2; *Chattanooga Daily Times,* December 19, 1908, p. 3.

[48] *Nashville Banner,* October 28, 1908, p. 1, and November 11, 1908, p. 2; *Chattanooga Daily Times,* January 24, 1909, p. 1.

En route to Ward's Hotel, the Riders halted at the farmhouse of Ed Powell and forced him to join the mob.[49] Powell, highly respected in the district, was the decoy that the masked men needed to insure an unimpeded entrance to the hotel. Upon arrival at the lodge, Powell informed Ward that several "fellows" needed to see his lawyer guests immediately. At that moment, half a dozen Riders forced their way past the stupefied Ward and hustled from room to room in search of their quarry. Other guests awakened in the melee were told to go back to sleep, and within minutes the intruders had roused the lawyers from their beds. Outside, Riders mounted on horseback poked their rifles through the lone window in the lawyers' room, thus discouraging the attorneys from any thoughts of escape.[50]

Imitating the voices of elderly, feeble women in a further effort to shield their identities,[51] the Riders ordered Rankin and Taylor to dress, including collar and tie, while a masked man brushed the dust from the attorneys' clothes, as if the lawyers were to attend a formal reception rather than a possible lynching.[52] After Fehringer had rummaged through their briefcases supposedly searching for significant papers, he scattered the contents around the room.[53] Some Riders said later that they sought no documents from the lawyers but that Fehringer's act involved intentional showmanship calculated to harass the captives.[54]

Rankin and Taylor were compelled to accompany the band on foot toward a slough that led off the main lake a quarter of a mile from the hotel. En route the Riders demanded that the attorneys promise relief from the court-enforced restrictions of the land company. The lawyers hesitated. When asked directly to reopen the lake to free public fishing, Rankin responded, "I couldn't possibly do that." [55]

---

[49] *McNairy County Independent,* December 25, 1908, p. 2; *Chattanooga Daily Times,* December 19, 1908, p. 1.

[50] Pinion interview and Morris interview.

[51] *Hickman Courier,* October 22, 1908, p. 1.

[52] *St. Louis Post-Dispatch,* October 21, 1908, p. 1; *New Orleans Times-Picayune,* October 22, 1908, p. 10.

[53] *McNairy County Independent,* December 25, 1908, p. 2; Taylor interview.

[54] Morris interview.

[55] Personal interview on October 21, 1956, with Jim Caksackkar, an ad-

Challenged by the uncompromising attitude of the lawyers, who probably believed they could talk their way out of the difficulty, the mood of the mob sharply veered from verbal bullying to determined vengeance. "Get the rope," a leader ordered as the band reached the slough. As the noose was fitted around Rankin's neck, a Rider shouted, "Give him time to pray."

"Gentlemen, I've already attended to that," replied Rankin. With that the lawyer was hoisted. "Gentlemen, don't do that; you're killing me," gasped Rankin.

"Damn you, that's what we intend to do," came the reply.[56]

Rankin was lowered and hoisted several times. Each time his would-be executioners demanded a compromise on the fishing question in return for his life. Rankin remained adamant.[57] Then, as he hung, a shotgun blast suddenly ripped into Rankin's body. More shots followed.[58] The hangman finally allowed the corpse to fall to the ground, and as a last indignity a Rider smashed the dead man's teeth with his rifle butt.[59]

The Riders then began to debate the fate of Taylor. Some argued that one murder was enough to prove the earnestness of their intention to "free" Reelfoot Lake. Others rebutted that Taylor could not be spared for fear he could identify his partner's assassins to the authorities. Taylor, squatting among several guards, listened to the exchange. As the Riders inclined more toward murdering than releasing him, Taylor broke for freedom.[60] He leaped into the slough and swam underwater for his life. The Riders fired their weapons into the water and at the surrounding banks for ten or fifteen minutes. Then, believing no human could have escaped such a fusillade, they prepared to leave. Garrett Johnson warned the Riders to burn their regalia and speak to no one of the night's activities.[61]

---

mitted former Night Rider, who lived in Reelfoot region most of his life. Hereinafter cited as "Caksackkar interview."

[56] *The Commercial Appeal*, December 20, 1908, pp. 1–2.

[57] *The Commercial Appeal*, December 22, 1908, pp. 1–2.

[58] *Nashville Tennessean*, December 22, 1908, p. 1; Johnson interview.

[59] Morris interview.

[60] *The Sun*, October 22, 1908, p. 1; *New Orleans Times-Picayune*, October 21, 1908, p. 12; *New York Herald*, October 22, 1908, p. 1; and, *St. Louis Post-Dispatch*, October 21, 1908, p. 1.

[61] *Chattanooga Daily Times*, December 22, 1908, p. 2.

Powell, who had been detailed to guard the horses of the Riders while Rankin was being tortured, slipped away during the confusion caused by Taylor's escape and reported the happenings to Ward and others.[62] They had heard the volley of shots but had not budged from the hotel for fear of involvement with the Night Riders. It was nearly dawn before a group ventured to the site where Rankin's mangled body lay. They found no sign of Taylor, whose footsteps led into the slough but could not be traced out of it. Weeds on the far side had been mown by bullets, and the searchers surmised that the lawyer's body lay under the water, probably weighted down by bricks.[63]

Ward phoned his attorney in Union City to tell him about the tragedy. The news spread quickly, and reports of the affair soon became front-page news throughout the country. The *New York Herald* announced that, "Colonel Taylor's body was not found until nearly noon. He had been hanged to a tree in a dense wood almost a mile from where Rankin was slain, and his body also bore a score or more of bullet wounds." [64] The *Nashville Banner* stated that Rankin was found "not quite dead," but, "Taylor's body was found hanging from a tree literally riddled with bullets." [65]

The truth during those hectic hours alive with rumors was that Rankin was dead and Taylor missing. Several prominent citizens of the area, including Tom Wilson, a leader of the Night Riders, carried the young lawyer's body to Ward's to await a coroner's inquest.[66] Meanwhile, others searched for Taylor. The slough, some fifty feet wide and seven feet deep,[67] was thoroughly probed for his body but with no success. The surrounding woods also failed to yield evidence as to the fate of Taylor.

Governor Patterson, who was campaigning for re-election in Covington, West Tennessee, when news of the murder reached him, immediately posted a $10,000 reward, the maximum allowed by

[62] *New Orleans Times-Picayune,* October 21, 1908, p. 12; *Chattanooga Daily Times,* October 21, 1908, p. 3.

[63] *Nashville Banner,* October 20, 1908, p. 9.

[64] *New York Herald,* October 21, 1908, p. 1.

[65] *Nashville Banner,* October 20, 1908, p. 1.

[66] *McNairy County Independent,* December 25, 1908, p. 2; *New Orleans Times-Picayune,* December 19, 1908, p. 1, and January 3, 1909, p. 3.

[67] *Nashville Tennessean,* October 21, 1908, p. 8.

law, for identification of Rankin's murderers.[68] Circuit Court Judge
Joseph E. Jones was ordered to adjourn the session at Dyersburg
and prepare for a special term in Union City at which a grand jury
would be assembled to consider evidence not only about the murder,
but also about night riding throughout the Reelfoot area. Finally,
the governor ordered his adjutant general, Tully Brown, to call out
the state militia, the first time that such a call had been necessary
since the Civil War. Three companies of troops from Nashville
were to meet the governor at Samburg and two others from Memphis
were placed on alert.[69]

"I have offered the largest reward the law will permit for the
arrest and conviction of the assassins of Rankin and Taylor . . . ,"
the governor told Tennesseans by press release. "I have believed that
the military should be the last resort in a state governed by law, but
it has now come to where it is my duty as governor to use all power
at my command to restore order. . . ." He added that he would
abandon his campaign in order to supervise personally the investigation of the crimes.[70]

The governor's vigorous response to murder won nationwide approval. His "prompt and firm stand for law and order will undoubtedly check the spread of the night rider movement," editorialized
the *New York Daily Tribune*.[71] *The Constitution* (Atlanta) wrote,
"Governor Patterson has started out right in taking the night riders
by the throat." [72]

Some, however, suspected Patterson's motives. His campaign had
been lackluster and needed a sensation to assure his re-election. The
situation at Reelfoot was readymade for political gain. The Louisville
Courier-Journal noted, "It will doubtless be said by his political opponents that his activities [in supervising the investigation] were
planned to make political capital. His attempt, especially if it should
prove successful, should make political capital and plenty of it." [73]
The South Pittsburg Hustler stated: "Governor Patterson's action

68 *The Commercial Appeal,* October 21, 1908, p. 1.
69 *Ibid.*
70 *Ibid.*
71 *New York Tribune,* January 9, 1909, p. 6.
72 *Atlanta Constitution,* November 1, 1908, p. 4.
73 *Courier-Journal,* October 24, 1908, p. 6.

. . . has the approval of all law abiding people, and it is certain that his political interests have not suffered by his abandonment of his campaign for the more important duty of upholding the law. He has made by this action and not lost." [74]

Undoubtedly the governor had "made" by devoting full attention to the Reelfoot affair. Regardless of the manner in which he might react to the murder, he was certain to draw criticism from his opponents, who could argue either that he had overplayed his hand for political gain, or that he had failed to respond as vigorously as the situation demanded. Most likely, the murder of Rankin and disappearance of Taylor genuinely outraged the governor, and he was sincerely determined to avenge the crimes with every means at his disposal.[75] However, as the investigation wore on, the governor undoubtedly became aware of the political advantages involved. He made certain that he stayed in page-one headlines by personally interrogating suspects and releasing news to the press. The state militia and district attorneys were not the only assistants; his campaign manager also joined the governor at Reelfoot Lake.[76]

Later, when the initial excitement of the Reelfoot affair ebbed, reporters asked Governor Patterson embarrassing political questions about his lackadaisical attitude toward night riding troubles in the Clarksville tobacco district in comparison with his strenuous efforts at Reelfoot Lake.[77] For the present, however, the sensation caused by the Rankin murder masked any inconsistencies in the governor's reactions to night riding. As far as Reelfoot went, he could only augment his popularity by prosecuting the assailants of Rankin and Taylor. He remained on record as favoring public control of the lake, thereby asserting his concern for those in the Reelfoot region who had not turned to night riding.[78] Public sentiment continued to govern Patterson's political practices throughout the Rider affair.

[74] *South Pittsburg Hustler* (Marion County, Tenn.), October 30, 1908, p. 4.

[75] Personal interviews on December 8, 1956, with Mrs. T. B. Hooker of Memphis, a daughter of the governor, and Ham Patterson of Memphis, his son.

[76] *Nashville Banner*, October 29, 1908, p. 7; Marquis, *Uncle Remus's, the Home Magazine*, XXV (March, 1909), 21.

[77] *Nashville Tennessean*, February 3, 1909, p. 4.

[78] Miles interview.

Some persons, however, searching for the underlying causes of the Taylor-Rankin tragedy, criticized the governor for failing to take positive measures against night riding prior to the assassination, which, according to the *Chattanooga Daily Times,* had been "encouraged by the looseness with which the laws of the state against the mob have been held even by constituted authorities . . ." [79] *The Daily Picayune* of New Orleans felt Patterson's reward offer indicated "how weak has been the administration of the law against the desperadoes heretofore. The time for prompt and firm action was in the beginning of the night riding. Nothing was done, and now the outlaws have such control of the situation that they will defy all movements against them." [80]

Newspapers were generally uncompromising in demanding stern justice for the murderers of Rankin. *The Commercial Appeal* in Memphis editorialized, "The dastards who committed this crime must be hunted down and brought to justice . . . If they resist, they must be destroyed. If caught, they must be tried, and all who are found guilty must be hanged." [81] The *McNairy County Independent* said the murderers "should be exterminated without judge or jury, as they did their victims." [82] The *Atlanta Journal* proclaimed: "Night riding today is worse than barbaric: it is Russian. When cutthroats are to be dealt with—and cowardly cut-throats at that— there should be no shade of tolerance. There is a remedy for the night riders. It is a hemp rope justly but speedily noosed." [83] Finally, the *Nashville Tennessean* wrote, ". . . There can be no room for any thought but to hunt down the murderers and strike them with the extremest penalty of the law." [84]

Several newspapers, such as the *Atlanta Journal,* did not believe that a permanent cure for night riding lay in hanging the culprits and temporarily stationing troops in the disturbed district. "What's needed is a rural police force for districts where trouble is likely." [85] *The Sun* (New York) concurred stating: "There have always been

[79] *Chattanooga Daily Times,* October 21, 1908, p. 4.

[80] *New Orleans Times-Picayune,* October 21, 1908, p. 6.

[81] *The Commercial Appeal,* October 21, 1908, p. 6.

[82] *McNairy County Independent,* October 23, 1908, p. 1.

[83] *Atlanta Journal,* October 21, 1908, p. 8.

[84] *Nashville Tennessean,* October 21, 1908, p. 4.

[85] *Atlanta Journal,* October 26, 1908, p. 4.

sporadic cases of mob murder in the South, when an epidemic has not generally prevailed, and there will always be such cases until respect for the law is generally enforced by a system of rural police such as exists in Western Canada . . ." [86]

While not condoning the crimes of the Riders, other journals sympathized with, or at least recognized, the motives behind the Night Rider movement. "The murder of Captain Quentin Rankin . . . reveals an ugly state of lawlessness in which the right is not all on one side," wrote *The World* (New York).[87] The real cause of trouble at the lake was "the mercenary motives of a few lawyers," according to the *Hickman Courier*.[88] The *Nashville American* said it had "no sympathy with the movement to convert Reelfoot Lake into a private property and exclude the people from it unless they pay for the privilege. The Legislature should purchase the property and make it free to all Tennesseans . . ." [89] The *Nashville Tennessean* accused the *American* of "wild-eyed, slambang and whooptedoodle idiocy" in its stand, charging, "It is just such bloody and lawless goose gabbing . . . that helps to undermine respect for law . . ." [90] But the *Union City Commercial* supported the *American* saying it had refused to endorse drainage of the lake when Harris first proposed it, and believed the State should buy title to land under and around the lake and turn it into a public preserve.[91] *The New York Times* found an excuse, "or at least an explanation," for the crime in the ignorance of the perpetrators, and reported the grievance of the Riders "real enough for men of their stage of civilization." [92]

The general tenor of press comment concerning the crime was summarized by the *Chattanooga Daily Times*: "Injustice may have been done the people of the Reelfoot Lake region; if so, the appeal was to the courts . . . Those who seek to lessen the cruelty of this crime by any sort of systematic recital of the supposed provocation overlook the deadly harm they are doing society and organized government." [93]

[86] *The Sun*, October 22, 1908, p. 6.
[87] *The World*, October 29, 1908, p. 8.
[88] *Hickman Courier*, November 5, 1908, p. 2.
[89] *Nashville American*, October 21, 1908, p. 4.
[90] *Nashville Tennessean*, October 24, 1908, p. 4.
[91] Quoted in *Hickman Courier*, November 5, 1908, p. 2.
[92] *The New York Times*, October 23, 1908, p. 8.
[93] *Chattanooga Daily Times*, October 23, 1908, p. 4.

Many of the out-of-state newspapers had difficulty with the basic facts of the case as well as with their geography. The *Charleston News and Courier* (S. C.) placed Reelfoot in the eastern Appalachian mountains and criticized the Riders as mountaineers of East Tennessee.[94] Even *The New York Times* described the descent of the Reelfoot Lake assassins from "their mountain fastness" to show their contempt of "low land law." [95]

Some Kentucky newsmen, who had seen their state chastised by the Tennessee press for its "black patch" night riding, returned a measure of the same after the Rankin murder. Hickman's *Courier* had correctly identified the murderers of the Walkers as Tennesseans, to which the *Troy News-Banner* (Tenn.) had responded that there were no night riders in West Tennessee. "If the *Banner* will turn its glasses toward Walnut Log, Tennessee, it will find material nearer home to work on," chided the *Courier*.[96]

Newsmen, including staff members of larger Tennessee papers and special correspondents ordered to the scene by out-of-state journals, flocked to Samburg and its environs within hours of the murder. The remains of other Night Rider victims were invented in news print, including a surveyor and a guide.[97] While some papers positively identified the corpse of Taylor, posses continued their search for the missing attorney.

Meanwhile, Governor Patterson traveled in a specially guarded train to Union City, where he met the three companies of state militia, 114 men and officers, commanded by Colonel William C. Tatom, a longtime Tennessee journalist. Together they marched in battle formation over the twenty miles of dusty, deeply rutted roads to Samburg, fearing momentary ambush by the Riders.[98] On the opposite side of Reelfoot Lake, an even more dramatic scene was unfolding. An elderly man, his face scratched and bleeding, his hair and beard matted with leaves and thorns, stumbled onto a lakeside farm and mumbled to the tenant, "I'm Colonel Taylor. Get me some help." [99]

94 Quoted in *Nashville Tennessean*, October 29, 1908, p. 4.

95 *The New York Times*, October 23, 1908, p. 8.

96 *Hickman Courier*, October 22, 1908, p. 2.

97 *The Sun*, October 21, 1908, p. 1.

98 Taylor interview.

99 *Ibid.; Nashville Tennessean*, October 22, 1908, p. 1.

CHAPTER 4

THE STATE REACTS TO MURDER

THE ESCAPE OF R. Z. Taylor from the clutches of the Night Riders was the result of courage, desperation, and considerable luck. Posses scouting the area in which he had disappeared turned up no clues as to his fate. More than 100 funeral wreaths from friends who presumed him murdered like his associate, Quentin Rankin, decorated the Taylor estate in Trenton.[1] His son Hillsman, a recent graduate of Vanderbilt University, was organizing former schoolmates into still another search party.[2] Then came the remarkable news: Taylor, although physically and mentally battered, was safe.

Taylor recounted the story of his escape many times during the next few months, first to the governor and then to newspapermen, his family, and finally most dramatically to a packed courtroom as he faced the men accused of his attempted murder. At times the details varied, but as he told it, he had made a lunge for the bayou a few steps from the body of his comrade, while the Riders debated

[1] *The Sun,* October 21, 1908, p. 1.
[2] *Atlanta Journal,* October 25, 1908, p. 1.

what should be done with him (Taylor). Once in the water he had swum underwater a few yards until he nudged against the trunk of a partially sunken tree that had toppled into the slough, its branches mired in the bottom. Passing beneath the log, Taylor rose for air on the opposite side, so that the tree shielded him from his would-be assassins. He clung to the log for support; had it moved, he would have been discovered, but it held fast.

Recovering from their momentary confusion, the Riders sprayed the slough and surrounding area with shot. Bullets chipped away at the log which hid Taylor, but none found their mark. After fifteen minutes of continuous firing, the masked men assumed that Taylor had been slain in the darkness, and his corpse had settled to the bottom of the slough. So they dispersed.

Fearful that the Riders might return or that they had posted a sentry at the slough, Taylor remained fixed behind the log for more than an hour. When there was no hint of movement from the area, he cautiously mounted the bank to his rear and peered across the water toward the body of his companion Rankin. The mutilated form gave no indication of life, so Taylor stumbled off into the brush for a considerable distance until he collapsed. Awakened by a searing Indian summer sun, Taylor found himself hungry, thirsty, and bleeding from painful scratches which crisscrossed his body wherever the briars had found bare skin. Maintaining a vague sense of direction which carried him away from the Obion side of Reelfoot—away from known Night Rider territory—he staggered north and then west across the swamps and bayous which bred cottonmouth moccasins among their plentiful wildlife. By afternoon, he was delirious. Night Riders and other enemies in distorted ghostly forms stalked him in his hallucinations, and again he fainted.

A cooler night revived the former Confederate soldier and revitalized his determination. All during the night of October 20 he traveled an imprecise route through difficult country. Soon after dawn he emerged from the morass and came upon a farmer doing his early chores. Taylor feared the individual might be a Night Rider or a friend of the clan. Nevertheless, at the end of his endurance, and in need of immediate assistance, he shouted for help.

The man who responded was Luther Rankin, a tenant farmer working Lake County land owned by Judge Harris. Taylor's ordeal had lasted some thirty hours and he had traveled more than twenty-five miles of harsh terrain, but at its end he could hardly have stumbled into more friendly surroundings. After tending briefly to Taylor's needs, Rankin phoned the county sheriff with the good news. Then he took Taylor by wagon to old friends and professional medical attention in Tiptonville. On the way, a sheriff's escort met them, and a cheering crowd greeted the exhausted Taylor, his blue eyes still dazed and his beard matted, as he rolled into town.[3] Later, when he had regained his strength and aplomb, Taylor remarked, "I guess the world will regard me as lucky, but after all I simply played a little trick that anyone in the heat of battle with the odds against him might play." [4]

How Taylor managed to beat those odds is still not completely clear. He was a Mason, and some contend that fellow Masons among the Riders allowed him to escape when he flashed a secret Masonic signal.[5] Self-admitted Night Riders later insisted that there should be nothing equivocal concerning their intentions toward Taylor; they meant to hang him with the same rope used on Rankin. That he escaped was probably due to the carelessness of his guards and to the daring of the prisoner.[6]

"There are no stories in the history or legends of America that equal the story of Col. Taylor's escape safely from his captors," thought the *Nashville Tennessean*. "Daniel Boone or Simon Kenton never had more thrilling, hairbreadth escapes from the Indians in the pioneer days, and there was no soldier in the great war between the states that grazed closer to death and came forth unharmed than did Col. Taylor . . ." [7]

Once the murder of Rankin had become public knowledge, posses dedicated to avenging him had begun a fast-paced, at times ruthless, search of Rider territory for the murderers. Although the governor had called out the militia, the posses did not intend to wait for the arrival of soldiers to extirpate the Riders. The posses were not

[3] *Chattanooga Daily Times*, October 22, 1908, p. 3; *The Commercial Appeal*, December 20, 1908, pp. 1–2; and Taylor interview.

[4] *The Sun*, October 21, 1908, p. 1.

[5] Caksackkar interview.

[6] Morris interview.

[7] *Nashville Tennessean*, October 22, 1908, p. 8.

authorized to operate in Obion; they had not been requested by the county sheriff in accordance with the law. They knew, however, that Governor Patterson would insure that they were absolved of any legal infractions incurred while tracking down Reelfoot's clansmen. Thus the pattern was set. This was only the first in a long sequence of deliberate legal oversights which permeated the state's efforts to punish Rankin's assassins. Citizens from throughout West Tennessee banded together, usually by counties, into para-law enforcement groups and galloped to Obion County in the name of justice. Hillsman Taylor assembled twenty Vanderbilt classmates.[8] Only Obion's Sheriff Easterwood, never anxious to arrest friends and neighbors even if they were Night Riders, declined to act until he had received orders directly from Governor Patterson.[9] However, any shortcomings caused by Easterwood's hesitations were more than overcome by the eagerness of Sheriff C. H. Haynes and his Lake County posses.

Since the Riders had brutally whipped Squire Wynne for his "loose talk," Lake and Obion Counties had existed as neighbors in a state of undeclared war. Lake County men pledged that should harm come to another of its residents, harsh vengeance would be exacted upon the Night Riders, and they drained the county's hardware stores of their newest weapons and ammunition in expectation of a showdown.[10] Across the lake in Obion, a similar atmosphere prevailed. Armed men had visited the general store of Charles Phillips near Walnut Log and had purchased large supplies of provisions. As they departed, they warned Phillips to keep silent about the sales.[11] Undoubtedly, Phillips' visitors were Riders; the men of Obion and Lake counties were spoiling for a fight.

The execution of Rankin gave Haynes and his Lake County deputies their long-awaited opportunity to ride into Obion County and punish the Riders. The sheriff's posse was reinforced by irate citizens, such as the fearless Judge Harris and the outspoken newspaper editor, G. C. Thomas.[12]

[8] *Atlanta Journal,* October 25, 1908, p. 1.

[9] Easterwood interview.

[10] *New Orleans Times-Picayune,* November 24, 1908, p. 3.

[11] *Nashville Banner,* October 26, 1908, p. 1.

[12] *New Orleans Times-Picayune,* November 24, 1908, p. 3; Marquis, *Uncle Remus's, the Home Magazine,* XXV (March, 1909), 21.

The first suspect arrested was Tid Burton, a fisherman found in Samburg by Haynes' men.[13] They charged him with complicity in the whipping of Wynne and escorted him to the Tiptonville jail. En route, Burton half-heartedly confessed to his participation in the Rankin murder and implicated others, but he recanted by the time he reached jail.[14]

The possemen also arrested other suspects whose names had been furnished by Pinkerton detectives whom Harris had hired to unmask the Rider organization. For four months they had been at their undercover work and could list seventy-five men as active Night Riders.[15]

While Governor Patterson welcomed the assistance of the posses, he expected the state militia to do the major work in capturing Rankin's murderers and in crushing night riding. A general fear was also developing that the rambunctious posses might suddenly veer toward lynch law and vent their revenge indiscriminately on the Reelfoot populace; therefore, many citizens expressed relief when three companies of Nashville militia arrived in Union City by train on October 21. There the governor delivered a pep talk, urging the soldiers to terminate the anarchy which had persisted in the lake region.[16] Not only suspects in the Rankin case were to be arrested but also all persons believed to be Night Riders. The State authorities theorized that Rankin's murder was not a single, desperate crime, but the culmination of a vast conspiracy to control the region. This conspiracy theory implicated all Night Riders in the assassination of Rankin.[17]

As was the case with the posses, the militia could not legally work in Obion unless requested by Sheriff Easterwood. There had been no such request, but Patterson remedied this with a telephone call to the sheriff.[18]

[13] *Nashville Banner*, October 28, 1908, p. 7.

[14] *Ibid.*

[15] *Atlanta Journal*, October 22, 1908, p. 1; *Nashville Banner*, October 22, 1908, p. 1.

[16] Miles interview.

[17] *Ibid.; Atlanta Journal*, December 19, 1908, p. 2; and *Nashville Banner*, December 19, 1908, pp. 1 and 8.

[18] *Louisville Herald*, October 21, 1908, p. 1; *New Orleans Times-Picayune*, October 21, 1908, p. 12.

The mystery that shrouded the Night Riders caused considerable exaggeration of the size and armed capabilities of the band. Therefore, the twenty-mile march from Union City to Samburg was a nervous one for the inexperienced troops, who anticipated possible ambush. The militiamen did not realize that the Riders—or those remaining free of arrest—were disorganized and somewhat intimidated by the impending arrival of the soldiers and had no intention of challenging their approach.[19]

Arriving without incident, the soldiers erected their camp in a partially cleared area called Shaw's Park, adjoining Samburg proper. They outlined streets and pitched their tents. The interrogation tent and quarters for the governor and ranking officers occupied the center of the encampment. Nearby stood the prisoners' stockade, and a barbed wire fence cordoned off the entire post.[20] The authorities declared martial law, but it encompassed only the area of the military post and was designed to discourage escape attempts by prisoners. Martial law implied swift military justice for suspects who did not co-operate. Also, Patterson desired to conduct the arrest phase of his campaign against the Riders in accordance with strict military codes and then rely on civil courts for the prosecution which would follow.[21] The Tennessee governor remained politically attuned throughout the Night Rider episode, and he realized that military justice, except for emergencies, would be unpopular with his constituency.

Detachments of soldiers, using natives as guides, immediately fanned out over the area. They made no distinction in their arrests between suspected Riders and innocent residents. All men, and some boys, were brought in for questioning. Little force was needed because most suspects came willingly.[22] Joe Johnson, later an admitted Night Rider, hurriedly buried his hood and gown in an orchard when troops arrived to question him. "They searched the coffee pot, under the mattress and everywhere for evidence I was a member of the

---

[19] Morris interview and Johnson interview.

[20] Personal interview on November 20, 1956, with Ben Capell of Memphis, who commanded contingents of Memphis militia sent to Reelfoot Lake during the night riding episode. Hereinafter cited as "Capell interview."

[21] *The Sun,* October 23, 1908, p. 5; *Nashville Banner,* October 24, 1908, p. 11; and Miles interview.

[22] Capell interview.

gang, but they never found any." [23] The soldiers arrested Johnson anyway. Throughout the investigation the militiamen found little material proof to implicate individuals. Apparently Rankin's assassins had heeded the instructions of Garrett Johnson to burn their regalia.

Arresting officers at times employed subterfuges to capture suspects. Bob Rankin, a member of the Lake County posse, told eight men that the governor wished to confer with them about their troubles at the lake and solicit their advice about solving them. But when the eight arrived at the military post, officially named Nemo by Colonel Tatom, they were arrested by militiamen and consigned to the prisoners' stockade. [24]

Though arrests were often arbitrary, camp officials attempted to sort out suspects once they had been interrogated. They released some in their own recognizance, although the local people remained liable to rearrest as investigations produced new evidence. John Cochran, who lived on an island in the lake, had been freed after questioning and had started home in his skiff when Sheriff Haynes, standing on shore, associated Cochran with the Wynne whipping. An exciting chase ensued. Cochran could pull an oar, but Haynes had commandeered a gasoline-powered launch. Spectators on shore cheered either Cochran or Haynes, depending on their sympathies in the Night Rider affair. Finally, Haynes overtook and re-arrested the suspect. [25]

A number of wanted men, however, did escape to other regions: eight men boarded a steamboat and crossed the Mississippi River to Missouri; several others fled to Central America. [26] The prosecution later was forced to delay publication of several night riding indictments returned by grand juries, pending arrests of the suspects charged. [27] Whether or not these defendants were ever arrested is not clear; however, their cases never went to trial. On the other hand, authorities did not confine their search to the Reelfoot district. They

[23] Johnson interview.

[24] *Nashville Tennessean*, October 25, 1908, p. 1; *Nashville American*, October 30, 1908, pp. 1 and 9.

[25] *The Sun*, October 23, 1908, p. 5.

[26] *New York Tribune*, October 24, 1908, p. 5; *The New York Times*, October 23, 1908, p. 4; *Nashville Banner*, October 26, 1908, p. 1; and Lasater interview.

[27] *Hickman Courier*, February 4, 1909, p. 4.

caught Robert George in Blytheville, Arkansas, and returned him to Obion.[28] Tom Ferrell of Hornbeak was arrested while watching an opera in Union City.[29] Indications are that the State successfully apprehended nearly all of the active Riders, including the leaders of the clan and those directly responsible for the death of Rankin.

Those retained as night riding suspects remained calm, if not cocky, in the face of the fast-paced investigation going on around them. They appeared certain that the State would not be able to construct a sound case against them. First, they foresaw the problem of collecting material evidence against the clan and believed that the membership would adhere to the oath of secrecy. Then, if all else failed, they still held the trump card: the Obion County jury which would "never" convict. At times the captives were arrogant. Frank James, held as a leader of the clan, chided his interrogators that he was a relative of Frank and Jesse James.[30] Bud Morris called the militia "just a bunch of kids," and averred that, "The Night Riders could have handled them anytime they felt like it, and those boys knew it." [31]

What the prisoners did not realize was that evidence, though scattered and as yet insufficient for trial purposes, was piling up against them. The militia had uncovered a ballot box purportedly used by the Riders to select their members and had taken crude masks, fashioned out of meal sacks, from several men in custody. Residents had begun to surrender themselves to the authorities,[32] and it appeared that the organization had begun to collapse, although loyalty to the fealty oath remained firm. What the State needed was a confession, and fortunately for its case, it possessed the means to obtain it: reward money, coercion, and promises of immunity from prosecution.

Although the military seemed to be in command, there were persistent reminders that the situation in Night Rider country lacked total security. The Memphis *News-Scimitar* reported, "It is openly stated by residents that a stranger takes his life in his hands if he

---

[28] *Nashville Banner,* October 27, 1908, p. 7.

[29] *Ibid.,* October 24, 1908, p. 11.

[30] *New York Tribune,* November 7, 1908, p. 3.

[31] Morris interview.

[32] *Atlanta Journal,* November 1, 1908, p. 2; *Nashville Banner,* October 27, 1908, p. 7.

undertakes to spend a night near the scene of the murder of Captain Rankin . . . If a man doesn't keep his mouth shut now, he might as well say goodbye to this world." [33] On one occasion, citizens reported twenty-five Night Riders had formed to attack Union City. "Scouts were sent out . . . and an investigation showed there was not a bit of foundation to this report." [34] Sympathizers of the Riders jeered Governor Patterson in Samburg and warned he would never live to see another election day.[35] Threatening anonymous mail was sent to the governor in Nashville.[36] Even at the funeral of Rankin in Trenton grief was mixed with alarm when three strangers appeared at the church and sat in a rear pew until the building started to fill with mourners. Then they quietly left, mounted their horses, and after inspecting the scene, departed the city.[37]

A Trenton doctor, T. J. Happell, found an unsigned letter on the steps to his office in which the authors proposed to "give Trenton hell and make away with the women, both Negro and white." Trenton would be visited the last of October, and "the people soon would be drinking water in hell." [38] One masked man halted a traveler and questioned his business in Obion. Another demanded breakfast of a farmwife and hid in nearby woods while she prepared it.[39] Obion's Attorney General D. J. Caldwell, prosecutor of Night Rider cases, received threatening mail [40] and in several locations the $10,000 reward notices seeking information in the Rankin case were replaced by handmade placards warning that Governor Patterson would be kidnapped unless he and the troops left the vicinity.[41]

The succession of threats and the evidence of continuing Rider activity unnerved many of the militiamen, especially those on night guard duty. They suspected that a horde of Riders was assembling to invade the camp and free their comrades. Colonel Tatom doubled

---

[33] *News-Scimitar,* October 22, 1908, p. 1.

[34] *The Commercial Appeal,* October 26, 1908, p. 2.

[35] *Courier-Journal,* October 24, 1908, p. 3; *Chattanooga Daily Times,* October 24, 1908, p. 1; and *The New York Times,* October 25, 1908, p. 11.

[36] *New Orleans Times-Picayune,* November 6, 1908, p. 8.

[37] *The Commercial Appeal,* October 26, 1908, p. 2.

[38] *New Orleans Times-Picayune,* October 27, 1908, p. 7.

[39] *Chattanooga Daily Times,* October 27, 1908, p. 2.

[40] *Nashville Tennessean,* October 22, 1908, p. 8.

[41] *Ibid.,* October 23, 1908, p. 1.

the guard and gave orders to "shoot to kill and show no quarter in case of attack." [42] The sentries took him at his word. They presumed any movement in the darkness to be a Rider, and several dozen milk cows paid the penalty for nervous trigger fingers. One picket fired at a dog, another at a hog, and a third at a line of stumps in the lake which he mistook for silently approaching Night Riders. Sleep during the early days at Nemo was always restless and frequently interrupted by rifle shots. One sentry was startled by the call of a crane to its mate and promptly called out the guard.[43]

Because of this general apprehension, Governor Patterson activated the two companies of Memphis militia that had been placed on alert. Posters on downtown Memphis buildings notified the men and within a day the Frazier Guards and Forrest Rifles had assembled under Major E. B. Horton and Captain Ben Capell. Heavy rain greeted the Memphis troops as they arrived by train in the town of Obion. Unable to persuade local citizens to guide them the fifteen miles through Night Rider country to Camp Nemo, they struck out on their own. Soon the main body of troops became separated from its trailing wagon train, but after circling aimlessly through foggy darkness the two units suddenly confronted one another. Each suspecting the other was a Night Rider contingent, a battle seemed imminent. However, a sentry challenged his adversaries, and the man who stepped forward to be recognized was his commander, Ben Capell.[44]

Arrival of the Memphis militia permitted the State to release the county posses which had been assisting in the manhunt. Then the Memphis reinforcements were quickly fitted into the routine at Nemo. The search for suspects continued. One military scouting party reached Spout Springs, "corralling the natives in herds like sheep, the soldiers standing with bayonets fixed and ball cartridges in the chambers of their rifles." [45] The troops took half a dozen

[42] Capell interview.

[43] *Nashville Banner*, October 24, 1908, p. 1; *Louisville Courier-Journal*, October 25, 1908, p. 1. Also personal interview on November 21, 1956, with Ben James of Memphis, member of the Memphis militia at Camp Nemo; hereinafter cited as "James interview."

[44] Capell interview.

[45] *The Commercial Appeal*, October 26, 1908, p. 2.

individuals into custody at Spout Springs and released the others.

The militia also made several embarrassing mistakes. One posse crossed the state line into Kentucky, and the Tennesseans sent apologies to Governor Willson of the neighboring state.[46] Soldiers arrested James Bryce, editor of the *Troy News-Banner,* a friend of Governor Patterson and an outspoken foe of night riding. They brought Bryce to Nemo, where he was immediately released with regrets. Bryce, however, remained indignant. He later reported that sixteen to eighteen soldiers had surrounded his office and ordered him to "dry up" while preventing him from phoning friends in Union City for advice. "All you Obion County people are guilty till you prove your innocence," the commander of the detachment warned Bryce. "If you don't go [with us], we'll shoot you." [47] The statements were indicative of the attitude of the militia toward the local people.

Despite the harsh words, the soldiers employed little brute force in pursuing their work. While the residents resented the high-handed tactics of the Lake County posse, they generally received the soldiers well, except for an occasional scowl. Several, such as Samburg's postmaster, offered to reveal the names of suspected Riders to the authorities.[48]

A windy coldsnap lowered temperatures at Camp Nemo into the forties in late October. Although it caught the soldiers in summer khaki uniforms and low quarter shoes and short on overcoats and blankets, morale remained good.[49] Louis "Red" Hasslock and Captain C. A. Bellamy of the Nashville troops displayed their virility by swimming in the lake.[50] Hasslock was a favorite at the camp. A 200-pound star right guard on Vanderbilt's football team, his fans asserted that "Red" would make mincemeat of the Night Riders.[51] But when his coach beckoned, "Red" went—walking twenty miles through Rider country to catch a train for Nashville so that he could travel with his teammates to Ann Arbor for their important inter-

46 Capell interview.

47 *Dresden Enterprise* (Dresden, Tenn.), November 6, 1908, p. 2.

48 *Nashville Tennessean,* October 24, 1908, p. 6; *Nashville Banner,* October 27, 1908, p. 7.

49 *Nashville American,* October 25, 1908, p. 2, and October 29, 1908, p. 1.

50 *Nashville American,* October 25, 1908, p. 2.

51 *The Commercial Appeal,* October 24, 1908, p. 11.

sectional game with the University of Michigan (which Vanderbilt lost, 24-6).[52]

Other heroics occurred. Ernest Rice, distinguished Dyersburg lawyer and former speaker of the Tennessee State Senate, volunteered to serve as a private in the ranks of the militiamen, and did so in the same corduroy suit he normally wore while hunting in Montana.[53] Soldiers who had missed the hurried calls to duty later filtered into camp. To get there they rode in open coal cars, hid in box cars, and walked for miles in inclement weather through unfamiliar territory to reach Nemo. Colonel Tatom allowed them all to stay on.[54]

The soldiers worked a long day. First call awakened the men at 5:55 o'clock and reveille was five minutes later. Taps sounded at 9:35. Sentries worked in twenty-four-hour shifts, two hours on duty and four off.[55]

Duty at Nemo, however, was far from all labor. During regular recreation periods the men played touch football or fished in the lake. Actually, official permission to hunt or fish was required, but the requisite was normally ignored.[56] As a safety precaution, officers did attempt to prevent game hunting with rifles. The young soldiers, many still in their teens, knew a minimum about handling their new Springfield rifles that could kill at two and one-half miles.[57] True sportsmen, however, could hardly suppress the temptation to hunt on a lake so laden with game. One day eight soldiers raised such a persistent rifle cannonade in pursuit of ducks that Colonel Tatom had them arrested, but he later released the militiamen with a warning.[58]

Under the circumstances, accidents were unavoidable. Captain Capell said, "We were our own worse enemies, and it's a wonder more didn't happen." [59] While attempting to close the chamber on his .45 caliber pistol, Lieutenant Dempsey of Nashville shot his

[52] *New York Tribune,* October 30, 1908, p. 4.
[53] *Nashville Banner,* October 24, 1908, p. 11.
[54] *Ibid.;* Capell interview.
[55] *Nashville Banner,* October 26, 1908, p. 3.
[56] *Nashville American,* October 29, 1908, p. 1; Capell interview.
[57] *Nashville Banner,* October 24, 1908, p. 11; Capell interview.
[58] *Nashville American,* October 29, 1908, p. 1.
[59] Capell interview.

buddy, Bradley Felts, in the knee.[60] Private Beecher Clark was cleaning his rifle in his tent when the weapon discharged and fired a bullet into a group of Memphis boys huddled around a fire. Corporal Allen Leftwich was wounded in the arm and Sergeant Howard Rutledge was killed when struck in the chest.[61]

Gloom caused by such mishaps did not last long, and despite the inhospitable weather, the normal atmosphere of the camp more resembled that of a picnic than that of a military post. Good food helped. Initially, a shortage of cooks existed, but Colonel Tatom directed Sheriff Haynes to impress half a dozen blacks as cooks. Haynes was given authority to arrest those who refused to serve.[62] Many soldiers regularly supplemented their diets with fish and game they caught and then cooked over campfires.[63] At regular meals served by the military they ate bacon, potatoes, bread, and coffee for breakfast and supper. The noon menu was the same except for beans and tomatoes on the side. Fish and duck were served on alternating days at one of the meals. Officers' mess was somewhat better than that allowed the enlisted men.[64]

The soldiers, sleeping eight to twelve to a tent, often preferred a pallet of straw to a cot because straw was warmer.[65] Prisoners had it worse. With little regard for sanitation and none for comfort, they were crowded—up to forty-seven at one time—into twelve-by-fourteen-foot tents, where they curled together on a thin layer of straw, which more often than not was soaked with rain water that had seeped under the tent.[66] Fires burned constantly in the dirt streets facing the tents, and soldiers as well as prisoners usually spent as much of their nights around the fires as they did inside their tents.[67]

Even as the investigation progressed, the military learned little about the true strength and organization of the Night Riders. The

[60] *Nashville Banner*, November 2, 1908, p. 1.

[61] *Ibid.*, November 7, 1908, p. 1.

[62] *Nashville American*, October 26, 1908, p. 1.

[63] *Nashville Banner*, October 27, 1908, p. 7.

[64] *Nashville American*, October 29, 1908, p. 1.

[65] *Nashville Banner*, October 30, 1908, p. 1.

[66] *Atlanta Journal*, October 29, 1908, p. 9; Morris interview and Johnson interview.

[67] Morris interview and James interview.

lack of information led commanders to take extraordinary precautions in guarding the post. Of the 300 soldiers in the camp, some nights fully half stood guard.[68] Reports that Riders were active in the area caused Colonel Tatom to surround Camp Nemo with three picket lines, the number he considered necessary to safeguard the governor and the prisoners. Of all the military operations at the post, sentry duty was considered the most important. Failure to fulfill guard duty was one of the few infractions that drew punishment; offenders were usually restricted to the camp area. Guards were ordered to challenge everyone, even friends they knew, a regulation which led to some levity. On one occasion, Hillsman Taylor confronted his frequent companion and superior officer, Captain C. A. Bellamy, who was in charge of the guard that night. "Advance," said Taylor, his weapon in a challenging position, and after a slight hesitation—"and give me a cigarette." [69]

Open house was held Sundays at the camp, and visitors came from within a fifty-mile radius to witness the unique scene on the shores of the lake. Among the first to arrive was Squire Wynne, the Lake County hunchback who had been cruelly whipped by the Riders in late April.[70] Fruits, cake, and jellies were brought to prisoners by their kin, and they were permitted to picnic together, as long as they stayed within earshot of a guard.[71] So many spectators arrived that one soldier hung out a "Standing Room Only" sign.[72] Possemen from surrounding counties who were assisting the militia in arresting suspects promised to bring young ladies from their respective communities to the camp on visiting days, but the soldiers complained that there were never enough girls to go around.[73] Many parents of youngsters in the lake region did not care to have their daughters consorting with the soldiers. The one exception was the Saturday afternoon dances arranged for the militiamen in Samburg. From that affair the soldiers usually escorted the girls to their homes. At one such dance, however, a local citizen in accord with the Riders

[68] *St. Louis Globe-Democrat*, October 26, 1908, p. 1.

[69] *Nashville Banner*, October 29, 1908, p. 7.

[70] *Ibid.*, October 26, 1908, p. 3; *New York Tribune*, October 26, 1908, p. 1.

[71] *Nashville American*, October 30, 1908, p. 9; *Nashville Banner*, October 26, 1908, p. 3; and *Atlanta Journal*, October 29, 1908, p. 9.

[72] *The Commercial Appeal*, November 2, 1908, p. 7.

[73] Capell interview and James interview.

offered a new dress to the girl who refused the request of a soldier to walk her home after the dance. Mrs. Seymour Osborne, then sixteen, remembered that she won that dress, "though it broke my heart. We all liked the soldiers." [74] The boys tore buttons off their uniforms and gave them to their girl friends as souvenirs, and several such buttons still remain in the possession of Reelfoot residents. One courtship that began informally at a Reelfoot dance culminated in the marriage of a young soldier from Nashville to a sixteen-year-old girl who had never traveled outside the lake region. [75]

Fraternization with the prisoners was prohibited by camp regulation, but the soldiers often did so under cover. [76] The city boys enjoyed the simple rural ways of the prisoners, and they allowed the suspects to warm themselves around their fires and in other ways befriended them. [77] The troops also enjoyed heckling or frightening the poorly educated, gullible prisoners. One prank was to toss blank cartridges into fires near the prisoners' stockade. The resultant detonations sent the suspects scurrying for cover. Once the militiamen lined up fifty prisoners before a mock firing squad and went through the motions of a formal execution. Hammers on the rifles fell with a click, but no bullets followed—only a flood of obscenities from the supposed victims. [78]

Harassing the prisoners, however, was only an occasional diversion among the soldiers. They generally busied themselves nursing sore feet, playing cards, writing letters home, and even building a zoo, whose captive animals included a fat pelican named "Nemo." [79] There was also considerable horseplay among the men. One group founded a so-called secret society, patterned after the Night Riders, which met at night and ordered comrades to do nonsensical things like walk into the lake while in uniform. [80] Indian war dances, stimulated by moonshine liquor, were now and then occurrences in the company streets. [81]

Because they anticipated only a short-term duty, the soldiers had

---

[74] Personal interview on November 16, 1956, with Mrs. Seymour Osborne.

[75] *Chattanooga Daily Times,* December 31, 1908, p. 1.

[76] Morris interview and James interview.

[77] Capell interview and James interview.

[78] James interview; Osborne interview.

[79] *The Commercial Appeal,* November 3, 1908, p. 2.

[80] *Nashville Banner,* October 30, 1908, p. 11.

[81] *Ibid.,* November 3, 1908, p. 6.

not included shaving gear in their personal equipment. When their beards began to show, a newsman reported that there was only one razor in the entire camp and that the men were beginning to resemble a detachment of Russian infantry. This caused the command at Nemo to hire a barber from Hornbeak to serve the camp. Nevertheless, washing and shaving still remained a chore, more often neglected than not.[82]

Colonel Tatom also attempted to be accommodating when the men had personal problems at home. He practiced a liberal leave policy. At the same time, he asked employers of the young men to display their patriotism by giving the militiamen leave with pay.[83] Prisoners also received considerations. William Caksackkar was paroled for one day to attend his wife's funeral, although his three sons, also in custody, were not permitted to go, a restriction which some newsmen thought unfair.[84] However, precautions were necessary because several prisoners had taken advantage of favors extended them to escape. Harry McQueen, for example, was permitted to accompany a friend to a doctor in Walnut Log, and while there eluded the soldiers who were their escort. McQueen then evaded prosecution by fleeing to Mississippi, where he worked for a year under an assumed name before returning to the Reelfoot region.[85]

Newspaper coverage of the Reelfoot affair was thorough, if not always accurate. Nine dailies had staff men at Nemo, including papers from St. Louis, New York, Cincinnati, Chicago, Memphis, and Nashville.[86] Others relied on their "stringers" in the area, those local persons retained on a commission to report events from their region. The reporters, who liked to call themselves "war correspondents," co-operated with one another in piecing together routine daily stories, but competition for the unusual feature and scoop was keen. Events occurred so swiftly that reporters in their eagerness to gather all the details often erred in their facts. Any retractions of such blunders lay well buried in the following day's article. Besides the error

---

[82] *Nashville American,* October 30, 1908, p. 9; *Nashville Banner,* October 29, 1908, p. 7.

[83] *Nashville Banner,* October 26, 1908, p. 3.

[84] *The Commercial Appeal,* October 30, 1908, p. 2.

[85] McQueen interview.

[86] *Nashville Banner,* October 27, 1908, p. 7.

which a number of papers made in pronouncing Taylor dead, when, in fact, he was in the midst of a spectacular escape, Memphis newspapers needlessly shocked their readers when they mistakenly reported Patterson had been assassinated by the Riders,[87] and the Mobile press reported a pitched battle between soldiers and Riders which never occurred.[88] Background stories frequently attributed to the Riders more than their share of crimes. Memphis' *Commercial Appeal* stated that the Riders at the height of their power had forced Samburg's mayor from office, but during that period Samburg had no mayor.[89]

Details, such as names of prisoners, the progress of interrogations, and future plans of the military and prosecution, were released by Governor Patterson and Colonel Tatom at regular press conferences, although they would answer specific questions anytime they could be found. Besides being commanding officer of the encampment, Tatom was associate editor of the *Nashville American,* and he understood the problems of newsmen covering a fast-breaking story. Therefore, he censored little (mainly items important to security) but he insisted that reporters refrain from interviewing prisoners and ordered his officers to withhold information concerning apprehended suspects until reports had been made to the commanders.[90] A Memphis reporter was arrested when he attempted to induce a private to enter a prisoner's tent in order to obtain the names of newcomers, but nothing came of the incident.[91]

Because of the prejudices of reporters and their papers, as well as the fact that sources of news were officially restricted, news content was heavily weighted in favor of the State. Correspondents made little effort to analyze the basis of the conflict from the standpoint of the natives. Wire service stories, used nationwide, carried the same biases. Many of the rural West Tennessee weeklies declined to offer any editorial comments on the happenings at Reelfoot, although they well understood the reasons for night riding.

[87] *Chattanooga Sunday Times,* October 25, 1908, p. 1.

[88] *Atlanta Journal,* November 1, 1908, p. 2.

[89] Personal interview on November 18, 1956, with Will Tidwell, who lived in Samburg in Night Rider days, substantiated by other Samburg residents of the same period.

[90] Capell interview.

[91] *Nashville American,* October 29, 1908, p. 1.

A lack of wire communications at Samburg contributed to the problems of reporters. When Camp Nemo was established, only a single telephone line ran from Samburg to Union City. Subscribers used it as a co-operative party line. At first, the State was forced to use the same line in order to communicate with Union City, and then via Union City to other points. Residents along the party line listened freely to the State's comments on the progress of the investigation. They overheard the plans of the prosecution and passed them on to whom they pleased before such plans could be implemented. Because of the heavy use of the single line, newsmen needed Colonel Tatom's permission to wire their articles through the telegraph office in Union City to hometown papers.[92] "Unfriendly" reporters could have been denied use of the telephone. Although there were no complaints that this occurred, the implied threat of censorship was always present.

After almost a week of near isolation, the military field telephone corps stretched a new line from Nemo to the Illinois Central Railroad station at Obion. Then the Cumberland Telephone Company provided new service from Nemo to Union City and direct telegraph connections from Union City to Memphis and Nashville.[93] The Obion connection was cut at night on several occasions, presumably by Riders or their sympathizers, but was quickly repaired the following day by mounted repairmen, who galloped spiritedly along the line until they located the break.[94]

During the early phase of the Reelfoot investigations, the press remained favorable to laudatory toward Governor Patterson. This attitude brightened his chances for re-election. "Governor Patterson's course in the Reelfoot Lake outrage proved him one of the biggest men the South has ever produced and gave him a national reputation," wrote the *Fayetteville Observer* (Tenn.),[95] while the New Orleans *Times-Picayune* noted that the action of Governor Patterson against the Night Riders "has gone far to re-establish him in

[92] *Atlanta Journal,* October 27, 1908, p. 1, and November 1, 1908, p. 2.

[93] *Nashville Banner,* October 26, 1908, p. 1.

[94] *Chattanooga Sunday Times,* October 25, 1908, p. 1; *Atlanta Journal,* October 24, 1908, p. 1.

[95] *Fayetteville Observer* (Fayetteville, Tenn.), November 5, 1908, p. 2.

general confidence and respect." [96] The *Nashville American* editorialized that the governor's decision to call out the militia spared the Reelfoot region from mob justice by preventing posses of vengeance-minded men from making indiscriminate arrests in the territory.[97] No political campaign the governor might have devised could have yielded the proceeds engendered by his activities at Reelfoot, and Patterson knew how to take advantage of his windfall. Campaign headquarters were, in effect, moved to Camp Nemo. Thomas Lawler, who lived in Memphis and served as secretary of the State Democratic Committee, spent days at Nemo with the governor. Their discussions certainly were not confined to night riding. Lawler readily admitted that the Reelfoot affair "has certain political significance, and it means the almost certain election of Governor Patterson for another term." [98]

While the Reelfoot sensation politically assisted the governor, it doomed the gubernatorial aspirations of his Republican opponent, George N. Tillman. The Republican candidate labeled Lawler's remarks "in the nature of a confession that Governor Patterson's record had been such that it required a bloody tragedy to divert the people's minds from his past acts." [99] Tillman asked, "Is this one act to serve as a cloak to hide all former sins? " He complained that the press had elevated the Reelfoot matter to the proportions of a Chickamaugua, Gettysburg, or Shiloh.[100] However, Tillman's protestations, perhaps justified, could not compete for news space with the daily reports emanating from Reelfoot Lake. Patterson remained in the daily headlines with his news conferences at Camp Nemo. By comparison, Tillman's press coverage amounted to hardly more than a footnote.

The governor's first term had hardly been distinguished, although under any circumstances it would have been difficult for a Republican to dislodge any Democratic Party candidate in traditionally Democratic Tennessee. The possibility, however, had arisen in 1908

[96] *New Orleans Times-Picayune*, October 28, 1908, p. 6.
[97] *Nashville American*, October 31, 1908, p. 4.
[98] *Nashville Banner*, October 29, 1908, p. 7.
[99] *Ibid.*, October 30, 1908, p. 14.
[100] *Ibid.*

because the Democrats had divided themselves in a bitter primary fight between Patterson and former U. S. Senator Edward Carmack. Governor Patterson and his advisors well recognized the Reelfoot affair as a *cause célèbre* which could reunite the party. Therefore, Patterson had cancelled his campaign schedule, and while pleading for Democratic Party unity, had basked in the publicity streaming from the troubled Reelfoot area.[101] The *Nashville American* correctly observed, "Nothing has occurred to line up the Democracy [Democratic Party] of West Tennessee [indeed all Tennessee] more solidly for the governor than the night riding trouble." [102]

Even Governor Willson of neighboring Kentucky recognized the political bonus to be gained from the Reelfoot publicity. "Shoot down the man with a mask who comes to your home at night," he admonished Kentuckians, "and you will need no lawyer to acquit you." [103] He also promised, "I will furnish soldiers for the protection of any farmer anywhere in Kentucky who wants to raise tobacco next year if he fears night riders, and I will see that the law is upheld and that murder and night riding are stopped if I have to borrow a million dollars to do it." [104]

Several newspapers, while praising Patterson for his personal response to the murder, charged that the inattention of both his administration and those of preceding governors to mounting difficulties in the lake region had precipitated the anarchy. "Had Tennessee lawmakers done their full duty ten or fifteen years ago when the lake question was first agitated, and declared the lake public property, as it is," wrote the *Dresden Enterprise,* "there would be no need for martial law in that section, and Captain Rankin would not have been killed in such a horrible and brutal manner by a band of masked midnight assassins." [105] Many Tennesseans supported the stand of the *Enterprise* and advocated that during the 1909 session of the General Assembly, legislation be passed to permit state purchase of Reelfoot Lake.[106]

---

[101] *Chattanooga Daily Times,* October 26, 1908, p. 1.

[102] *Nashville American,* October 30, 1908, p. 9.

[103] *Louisville Herald,* October 27, 1908, p. 1.

[104] *New York Herald,* October 26, 1908, p. 5.

[105] *Dresden Enterprise,* October 30, 1908, p. 2.

[106] *Trenton Herald-Democrat* (Tenn.), October 29, 1908, p. 3.

Governor Patterson also favored state ownership of the lake, and when the legislature met in January, 1909, he pressed for laws which would bring Reelfoot under public control. First, however, night riding at the lake had to be crushed and its participants punished. At least three posses were ordered into the field each day to arrest more suspects. For some possemen it became a game. Who could capture the greatest number of Riders in a day? Or who could make the most important "catch"? A financial lure enlivened the competition. Under state law, sheriffs received one dollar for each criminal suspect arrested. Therefore, the Night Rider roundup afforded sheriffs the opportunity of earning a considerable bonus. Sheriff Haynes and his Lake County posse desired vengeance more than money and rarely allowed a lack of evidence to deter them from making an arrest. On the other hand, Sheriff Easterwood of Obion County sought financial profit. Haggling over the custody of prisoners led Haynes and Easterwood close to violence. At one point, Easterwood threatened to take an Obion prisoner from Haynes by force, but the farce ended short of tragedy when Haynes peaceably surrendered his charge.[107]

Ninety suspects, including several women, were in custody by the end of October,[108] and as specific evidence developed against individuals, they were categorized according to the strength of the case against them. Three identified as leaders of the band—Garrett Johnson, Tom Johnson, and William Watson—were consigned to solitary confinement.[109] Thirty-six, who gave satisfactory explanations of their activities to interrogators, were released in their own recognizance.[110] This group included P. C. Ward, owner of the hotel from which Rankin and Taylor had been taken,[111] and Fred Carpenter, the Union City lawyer at whose behest the victims came to Walnut Log. Governor Patterson warned the freed suspects that they would be recalled to camp if implicated by further evidence, or they could be ordered to appear before the grand jury as state witnesses. In

[107] *Nashville Banner*, October 26, 1908, p. 3; Easterwood interview.

[108] *Atlanta Journal*, October 29, 1908, p. 9; *Chattanooga Daily Times*, October 26, 1908, p. 1.

[109] *Atlanta Journal*, October 28, 1908, p. 1.

[110] *Nashville Banner*, October 30, 1908, p. 1; *Courier-Journal*, October 26, 1908, p. 1.

[111] *Chattanooga Daily Times*, October 30, 1908, p. 1.

either case, they were honor bound to comply, and if they did not, they would be rearrested and themselves face possible trial. The natives agreed to the stipulations outlined by Patterson, and after saying friendly goodbyes to the soldiers who had guarded them, they hurried away.[112]

Meanwhile, the prosecution and defense had begun to prepare for the inevitable trial. Defense attorneys were severely limited, however, by the refusal of the military to allow them to confer with their clients.[113] This constituted a highly unusual, if not illegal, restriction, but the State insisted that the abnormal situation in the Reelfoot territory demanded it. The prosecution needed confessions on which to build its case, and the State knew that the first admonition of defense lawyers to their clients would be to remain silent.[114]

The State shielded the nature of the evidence it was collecting in connection with the case. Enough information leaked out, however, to assure newsmen that a powerful case was being developed. As one search party carried a wagonload of prisoners back to Camp Nemo, a woman rushed to the gate of her home and in near hysteria cried, "Thank God the time has come when I can tell what I know." [115] The time had come for other more important witnesses to tell what they knew.

A special press conference called by the governor for October 30 portended an important new development. In a deliberate tone he informed newsmen, "We know who fired the [first] shot and who put the rope around Rankin's neck . . . . The State will have ample evidence to convict." [116]

Rumors had been circulating throughout the camp for several days that a ranking Night Rider had turned state's evidence. Now it was confirmed. A member of the band had broken his oath of secrecy; others were to follow.

112 *Nashville Banner,* October 30, 1908, p. 1.
113 *Nashville American,* October 31, 1908, p. 5.
114 *Ibid.*
115 *Chattanooga Daily Times,* October 27, 1908, p. 1.
116 *Ibid.,* October 31, 1908, p. 1.

CHAPTER 5

PRETRIAL LEGAL MANEUVERS

THE NIGHT RIDER who turned state's evidence and became the cornerstone of the prosecution's case against the entire band was Frank Fehringer, the petty bootlegger from Hickman, Kentucky. He admitted being a long-time Rider, even a leader of several of the organization's more sanguinary ventures. He had participated in the slaughter of the Walker family near Hickman and later the murder of Quentin Rankin at Walnut Log.[1]

Fehringer bared the secrets of the gang and surrendered its passwords, oath, and other rituals to the authorities. He named names: Tom Wilson was Rankin's hangman and Bob Huffman his assassin. Garrett Johnson had led the murderers.[2] After a three-hour grilling by the State's investigators, Fehringer had to be half carried by two of his guards to his solitary confinement tent one hundred yards away.[3]

[1] *The Commercial Appeal*, October 29, 1908, p. 1; *News-Scimitar*, December 21, 1908, p. 1.

[2] *Nashville American*, November 6, 1908, p. 1.

[3] *The Commercial Appeal*, October 29, 1908, p. 1.

News of the confession was received with immense satisfaction throughout the state. "The blood of Capt. Quentin Rankin, which has been crying aloud for vengeance from the lonely hollow below Walnut Log for the past week, has at last heard an echoing cry," wrote the *Chattanooga Daily Times,* "and justice, it seems, is about to gather into its hands the assassins." [4]

Why did Fehringer confess? The State insisted that his action was voluntary, and that Fehringer had sent for the governor saying he wanted to clear his conscience of night riding crimes. No reward money changed hands, but after his confession, Governor Patterson promised Fehringer immunity from Tennessee law and safe passage from the Reelfoot region to a new home in another part of Tennessee. [5]

Former Riders have their own opinions as to Fehringer's motivation. Fehringer had been jailed in Hickman on a bootlegging charge in the summer of 1908, and many Riders believed that Judge Harris paid his bail and then hired the affable 27-year-old wanderer to penetrate the Night Rider organization and learn its secrets. Fehringer then had won the confidence of Garrett Johnson, the chief of the Riders, and had become Johnson's lieutenant. [6] It was Fehringer who had led the raid on the Walkers, [7] and Fehringer who had lifted the masks of various Riders to check their identities at a meeting in Bogus Hollow. [8]

That Fehringer was a hired spy seems unlikely. No one designated him as such during the trials of the Riders, and although the defense contended that the State had bribed him to talk, it made no inferences concerning a relationship with Harris. Incomplete court records at Hickman reveal arrests for bootlegging and the illegal possession of side arms, but none places Fehringer in jail at the time of the Night Rider activities.

W. H. Swiggart, a prosecuting attorney in the Rider trials, insists no bribes or coercion persuaded Fehringer to talk. He believes that "Frank Fehringer was an exhibitionist who enjoyed the limelight,

4 *Chattanooga Daily Times,* October 29, 1908, p. 1.
5 *The Commercial Appeal,* December 22, 1908, p. 1.
6 Johnson interview.
7 Morris interview.
8 Hogg interview.

and it was his ego which induced him to become a state's witness." [9] This analysis of Fehringer's character was substantiated during the trial. He reveled in the witness chair as the star attraction of the proceeding. Arrogantly playing his role, he resisted a rigorous cross-examination and reprimanded defense counsel when the questioning made him uncomfortable.[10]

This is not to say that the State was beyond intimidation when questioning suspects. A favorite psychological prod was to show the rather ignorant and superstitious natives a coffin and warn them it would be theirs if they did not reveal the truth about the Night Riders.[11] Governor Patterson handed Bud Morris a hangman's noose and asked if he thought it would fit around his neck.[12] The blood-stained rope used to hang Rankin was tossed across the lap of Jim Caksackkar.[13] And the governor resorted to coarse, threatening language in questioning Harry McQueen.[14] All one night unknown parties stood outside the tent of William Russell, a suspect considered inclined toward confession, urging him to tell what he knew. They punched at his head through the canvas with "some hard substance," probably a rifle butt, while warning him, ". . . We found masks and arms at a [your] house and we know [that you know] all about it." [15]

While the State had employed some harsh means while trying to extract admissions in the first days of questioning, they were not needed once Fehringer's full confession exposed the organization. Following his disclosures several Riders willingly confessed their parts in the clan on the promise of a pardon and safe journey from the area.[16]

Tid Burton, the first suspect captured and quickly taken to Tiptonville by Sheriff Haynes and his men, also confessed about this time.[17] Burton had been sullen and even defiant in prison, but ap-

9 W. H. Swiggart, personal letter to the author, November 24, 1956.
10 *Nashville Banner*, December 22, 1908, p. 3.
11 Morris interview and Caksackkar interview.
12 Morris interview.
13 Caksackkar interview.
14 McQueen interview.
15 *Chattanooga Daily Times*, December 24, 1908, p. 1.
16 *Ibid.*, p. 7; Taylor interview.
17 *Chattanooga Daily Times*, October 28, 1908, p. 1.

parently tempted by the $10,000 reward and confident that the militia could protect him from reprisals by his fellow-Riders, Burton decided to talk.[18] He admitted participation in the burning of Shaw's fish docks at Samburg in April and in the thrashing of Squire Wynne that same month; however, Burton insisted that he had not been present at the Rankin murder, although he had helped to spread the word that the lawyers were headed for Walnut Log. He identified Tom Johnson, Garrett Johnson, and William Watson as leaders of the band,[19] and implicated others in night riding activities. After later repeating his confession for the State's attorneys, contradictions developed, and instead of serving as a witness for the prosecution and receiving a pardon for his crimes, Burton instead became a defendant along with the other notorious members of the gang.[20]

In any event, Burton's unreliable testimony was not crucial to the preparation of the State's case. Fehringer's confession had been substantiated by two other self-admitted Night Riders, Herschell Hogg and Wad Morris, who volunteered to talk in exchange for clemency.[21] It was a confident Governor Patterson who announced that the number of men active in the Rankin hanging probably did not exceed ten. Others had stood guard and held horses, but in all no more than thirty-three took part. Evidence was strong enough to assure their conviction.[22]

Other information concerning the activities of the band flowed continuously to the interrogators. For example, a Mrs. Keith revealed that her teen-aged son had been taken from their home near Hickman and forced to accompany the Riders in their attack on the Walkers. When Walker returned the rifle fire of the intruders, the boy had been killed and buried in a nearby forest. Because the Riders had threatened to punish her if she complained about the death of her son, the mother had remained silent until the militia could assure her of protection.[23]

---

18 *Atlanta Journal,* November 5, 1908, p. 8.

19 *Chattanooga Daily Times,* October 28, 1908, p. 1; *Nashville Banner,* October 27, 1908, p. 1.

20 *Nashville Banner,* December 21, 1908, p. 7.

21 *Chattanooga Daily Times,* October 31, 1908, p. 1.

22 *Ibid.*

23 *Courier-Journal,* October 29, 1908, pp. 1–2; *New Orleans Times-Picayune,* October 28, 1908, p. 3.

Obion County District Attorney D. J. Caldwell directed the prosecution of the Night Rider cases. For sixteen years a member of Tennessee's Supreme Court and a lawyer of excellent reputation, he had been threatened on numerous occasions during the previous six months for his energetic, often hampered, efforts to eliminate night riding in the Reelfoot district. Several cases involving whippings and other depredations had been brought to trial, but the inevitable result had been a hung jury.[24] Most observers believed that no jury impaneled in Obion County could ever be persuaded to convict the Night Riders, who were both feared for their potential cruelty and admired for their rash campaign to open Reelfoot Lake to public use. At times witnesses summoned to testify in court proceedings were whipped by the Riders and commanded not to appear. They seldom disobeyed. Garrett Johnson had issued the general order that anyone who did testify must be apprehended and hung.[25] Although harassed by this situation, Caldwell had continued to do his duty, and when Rankin was murdered, he was presenting evidence to the grand jury concerning house burnings and armed assaults attributed to the Riders.[26]

Governor Patterson placed the full legal facilities of the State at Caldwell's disposal. Assisting the district attorney were several notable attorneys, including W. H. Swiggart, Hal Holmes, Felix W. Moore, and Hillsman Taylor, son of the victim of the Riders. The prosecution anticipated the eventual trial of at least 100 defendants on night riding charges.[27]

The suspects were not long without competent counsel. Their kin and friends pooled finances to hire former U. S. Congressman Rice A. Pierce of Union City to protect the interests of the prisoners. Pierce already knew most of his clients, for he had defended them unsuccessfully in their earlier court struggles with Harris. The attorney also was a personal and political friend of Governor Patterson. Yet the alleged Night Riders had unqualified faith in Pierce.

[24] *Nashville Banner,* October 27, 1908, p. 7; personal interview in December, 1956, with Mrs. L. D. Killion, niece of Attorney General Caldwell.

[25] *New York Tribune,* December 22, 1908, p. 4; *Nashville Banner,* October 27, 1908, p. 7.

[26] Miles interview.

[27] *Ibid.;* Taylor interview.

They believed that he sympathized with their problems at the lake, and of even more immediate importance, understood the temperament of Obion County jurors.[28]

Following the Rankin murder, Pierce had received a note from the "Lake County Vigilance Committee" warning him not to defend the "damned rascals who whipped Esquire Wynne in Lake County," [29] but Pierce scoffed at such threats and vowed the prisoners soon would be free. "I'm not afraid of any jury they can get here," he declared, "and I'm going to free these men they have charged with the crime." [30] Pierce was considered the finest criminal defense attorney in the area. Although his technical knowledge of the law was mediocre, his oral presentations to juries and his courtroom theatrics were convincing enough to be nearly always successful.[31]

Assisting Pierce was his law partner, Joe Fry. They were opposites in skills and temperaments. Fry's arguments to a jury were legally sound and meticulously presented in a low-key monologue. Pierce thundered, cajoled, stretched legal ethics, and summoned tears in his emotional appeals to "reason." Fry prepared the legal briefs and counseled his partner on proper procedure. During trials he seldom rose to his feet other than to take legal exception to an adversary's statement. The Night Rider cases, however, would severely test them. Their legal opposition included the best the State could assemble. They also faced a strong public opinion which demanded that Rankin's murder be avenged.[32]

Pretrial planning and legal maneuvering exhausted November and half of December. Because the question of the composition of the jury remained crucial, the State decided to handle the cases of the Rankin murderers first. Then it could turn to those defendants, who, masked and at night, had raided the countryside in violation of the Ku Klux Klan Act.

Fehringer, Hogg, and Morris, three Riders who had confessed to the State, were escorted to jail in Memphis to prevent the possible "contamination" of the State's key witnesses by friends of the pris-

---

[28] Morris interview and Pinion interview.
[29] *Chattanooga Daily Times,* October 24, 1908, p. 2.
[30] *Nashville Tennessean,* November 9, 1908, p. 1.
[31] Miles interview.
[32] *Ibid.*

Quentin Rankin, murdered by the Riders

R.Z. Taylor, who escaped the Riders

Slough near Walnut Log, where the Riders hanged Rankin (marked by cross), and where Taylor escaped by swimming under water and then by hiding behind log (marked by arrow)

J.C. Burdick (below) owned the above fish dock at Walnut Log. Its sister dock at Samburg was burned by the Riders.

Judge Harris, principal owner of Reelfoot Lake and target of Night Rider hatred

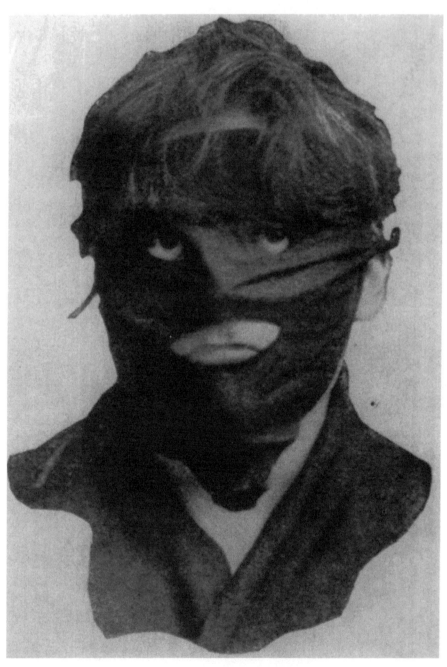

Night Rider masks generally were made from meal sacks and pointed at the bottom to resemble a beard.

H.B. (Con) Young was whipped by the Riders because he refused to sell his sportsmen's lodge to one of their friends.

Dr. G.C. Thomas, Tiptonville newspaper editor, defied the Riders and named them in print.

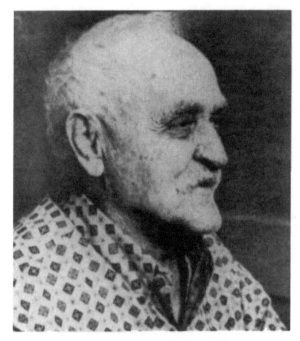

Fred Pinion, self-admitted Night Rider leader

Frank Fehringer, the State's star witness against his former kinsmen

Ella Pride (who boasted of being the only female Rider) turned state's evidence after being whipped by the clansmen

Tid Burton, first Rider arrested

A Lake County posse, including women, assembled to track down Riders

Forrest Rifles of Memphis, called to duty in Night Rider territory

Crowded courtroom in Union City (including militiamen to keep order)

Gov. Malcolm R. Patterson of Tennessee

Attorney General D.J. Caldwell (below) presented the State's case to Judge Joseph E. Jones (upper right) while Rice A. Pierce led the defense counsel

Two views of West Tennessee's Reelfoot Lake

oners.[33] Rumors that Tid Burton might be taken from the Tipton-ville jail by a Lake County lynch mob caused his transfer to jail in Union City.[34] Nine prisoners against whom the State believed it had its strongest evidence were transported to the Davidson County Jail in Nashville. These nine prisoners, labeled leaders of the clan, had been held in solitary confinement at Camp Nemo since their arrest, but all nine—Garrett Johnson, age forty-two; Tom Johnson (second cousin to Garrett), fifty-three; Roy Ransom, twenty-six; Bob Lee, thirty-six; Bob Huffman, twenty-six; Sam Applewhite, twenty-seven; Tom Wilson, forty-six; Jesse Carter, twenty-three; and Elijah "Lige" Cloar, forty—were considered directly involved in the execution of Rankin.[35]

Meanwhile, at Nemo the militia doubted that it had apprehended all of the Riders, and Major Horton reinvestigated a series of low-land areas where the Riders had previously been active. He was under orders to "shoot any masked man without calling him to a halt." [36] The order made newspaper headlines but seems incon-gruous with the operation as it was being conducted, for any Riders still at liberty certainly would not be wearing masks, and in making past arrests the military had shown restraint in the use of weapons. No militiaman shot a suspect during the entire Rankin episode.[37]

At this same time, the Obion County Grand Jury was meeting daily in Union City to assess evidence that might warrant indictments against the prisoners. Fearful that deliberations of the jury would be interrupted by marauding Riders, a special guard of fifty men had been organized to co-operate with Union City police in defense of the city.[38]

The jury itself was hardly representative of the area. Not one of the fifty men selected for jury panel duty by Sheriff Easterwood lived in the lake region of the county. All of the jurors had been out-spoken in their denunciation of night riding, although they swore

[33] *Chattanooga Daily Times,* October 31, 1908, p. 1.

[34] *Ibid.,* October 29, 1908, p. 1; *Courier-Journal,* October 29, 1908, p. 1.

[35] *Chattanooga Daily Times,* November 2, 1908, p. 1; *Nashville Tennes-sean,* November 2, 1908, p. 1.

[36] *Chattanooga Daily Times,* October 29, 1908, p. 1.

[37] Capell interview.

[38] *Chattanooga Daily Times,* October 27, 1908, p. 1.

they could disregard their personal prejudices and decide individual cases on the basis of the evidence presented.[39]

Judge Jones, who was given to emotional rhetoric (especially when it appeared verbatim in print), reminded the jurors in his opening statement to the panel: "The blood of Captain Rankin, which was shed upon the banks of Reelfoot Lake, at midnight's holy hour, by a band of men, alleged to have their faces covered to avoid detection, cries out for legal vindication and the punishment of the horrible act which has astonished the world. Our own Tennessee and the beautiful southland, where the purest and best strain of Anglo-Saxon blood flows through the veins of her people, is mortified and humiliated by the awful crime . . ." [40]

The pathos evoked by Judge Jones brought tears to the eyes of the jurors,[41] but more important, it indicated His Honor's attitude toward the proceedings. The judge wanted justice. He was a fair-minded jurist, but he also wanted indictments, convictions, and retribution. The law was not inflexible; it could be stretched and manipulated to meet the demands of a difficult situation. The judge soon proved that he understood these facts and had little compunction in using them to the State's advantage.

Several Nashville attorneys observing the proceedings believed that the grand jury was illegally in session, and that any of its findings could be voided by a superior court. State law required that thirty days public notice be given before a special grand jury, such as the one hearing the Night Rider evidence, could be seated.[42] Because of the pressure for speed in the Reelfoot investigation, Judge Jones had not done this. He had impaneled the jury with no notice whatsoever immediately after the murder. However, the State soon developed a solution to the problem. The present grand jury would continue its work, but a second special grand jury would be called for December in keeping with the thirty-day notification rule. Then the strongest evidence developed by the current jury would be quick-

[39] *St. Louis Globe-Democrat,* October 16, 1908, p. 1; *Courier-Journal,* October 26, 1908, p. 1.

[40] *Chattanooga Daily Times,* October 28, 1908, p. 2.

[41] *Nashville Banner,* October 26, 1908, p. 11.

[42] *The Sun,* October 28, 1908, p. 3; *Chattanooga Daily Times,* October 29, 1908, p. 1.

ly reintroduced to the new, legally seated panel and indictments drawn. Judge Jones concurred with the strategy, and on November 4 he scheduled a new grand jury session for December 7.[43]

Pierce attacked the State's case by seeking outright freedom for his clients on grounds they had been illegally arrested. He argued that the governor had acted unconstitutionally in calling out the militia without the authority of the legislature; therefore, arrests by the soldiers had been illegal. The defense did not expect this maneuver to win freedom for the Riders. Even if the court agreed with him, Pierce knew that the prisoners would be immediately rearrested by civil authorities. He did, however, hope to force the transfer of the cases from military to civil jurisdiction where the law concerning trial procedure was less strict.[44] As a test case, Pierce filed a motion with the court demanding the release of Will Watson, a respected farmer, with means of some $15,000, whose brother was the pastor of Union City's First Baptist Church.[45]

Realizing that his clients would not be freed regardless of the court's findings in the Watson case, Pierce, at this same time, also requested bail for all of the defendants. He noted that the alleged Riders had not even been charged with a crime, and that according to Tennessee law, only suspects charged with capital offenses could be denied bond.[46] Therefore, if the prosecution desired to oppose bail—and it certainly did—it would be forced to present sufficient proof in open court to sustain capital charges against the defendants. Even more than gaining freedom for his clients, Pierce wanted to hear this proof; it would give him a sure indication of the strength of the State's case against the entire clan. For its part, the prosecution was not loath to reveal evidence publicly because it might assist the defense. Instead it feared that further general publication of the facts would make it even more difficult to obtain a trial jury. It was the question of qualifying that jury that persistently harassed the prosecution.

The State, however, was left with little choice. If the bond issue

---

43 *Nashville Tennessean*, November 5, 1908, p. 2.

44 *Ibid.*, pp. 1–2.

45 *Nashville Banner*, October 31, 1908, p. 1; *Chattanooga Daily Times*, October 31, 1908, p. 1; and *New York Tribune*, October 31, 1908, p. 4.

46 *Nashville Tennessean*, November 5, 1908, pp. 1–2.

came to a hearing, it would have to produce the evidence necessary to hold the suspects without bail.[47] Governor Patterson prepared to testify as to the severity of night riding in the lake district and the need for drastic force to suppress it.[48] Fehringer, Hogg, and Morris, the three Riders who had turned state's evidence, would testify as to the activities of the clan itself.[49] The State's case might be weakened, but no other remedy appeared possible.

Before the matters came to a public hearing, the State sought a compromise with the defense. If Pierce desisted in this pretrial pleading, it would agree to a $5,000 bond for Watson. Furthermore, as Watson was already under $5,000 bail in connection with a Lake County charge that stemmed from the whipping of Squire Wynne, the bail could also stand for the Obion case. The prosecution also consented to a $25,000 bond for Ed Marshall, probably the most prominent and affluent of the suspects.[50]

Pierce accepted the bond proposals for Watson and Marshall but not the entire compromise. He demanded the release, at least on bail, of all the prisoners. In this regard, he continued to challenge the governor's legality in summoning the militia. It was a close legal question. The state constitution permitted the governor to assemble the state guard only in time of rebellion or invasion and then only upon authority of the General Assembly. But the legislature in 1893 had given the chief executive power to activate the militia in suppressing insurrections, mobs, and unlawful assemblies which local authorities could not control or which threatened the best interests of the state.[51] Seemingly the two provisions were in conflict.

In his arguments, Pierce's "voice rose to a high pitch and turning so that he faced the State's attorneys and not the court, he opened the vials of his ridicule and deluged them with its contents . . ." [52] But to no avail. Judge Jones upheld Governor Patterson's rights to summon the state militia under circumstances such as those which

[47] *Ibid.*, November 6, 1908, p. 1, and November 9, 1908, p. 1.

[48] *Ibid.*, November 6, 1908, p. 1.

[49] *Ibid.*, November 5, 1908, pp. 1–2.

[50] *Ibid.*

[51] *Ibid.*, November 7, 1908, p. 1; *Chattanooga Daily Times*, November 19, 1908, p. 1.

[52] *The Commercial Appeal*, November 8, 1908, p. 2.

had existed at Reelfoot Lake and ruled that the suspects were legally held by military authority.[53] Then turning to the question of bail for the prisoners, he said that he doubted that the evidence in the Night Rider cases should be examined publicly in court while the grand jury was in session investigating the same matters.[54] The prosecution had won the first court skirmish, and Judge Jones had well shielded the State's case from potentially weakening probes.

Pierce, however, did manage one success. In the midst of the bail hearing he unexpectedly petitioned Judge Jones for the right to counsel with his clients—a privilege normally accorded defense attorneys—but which had been denied Pierce by the military. He caught the State off guard, and the prosecution reluctantly agreed to Pierce's request even before the court ruled on the question. That evening, November 6, the attorney spoke to eleven of his clients for the first time since their arrest.[55]

Another startling event occurred in court that day. Thomas Southworth, Union City's lone professional photographer, had been given special permission by Judge Jones to take photos of the hearings from the rear of the courtroom. When Southworth ignited his powder flash, the whoosh of sound and the light that swept the courtroom created the instantaneous impression that friends of the Riders had tossed a bomb into the chamber. The incident sent some of Tennessee's more able attorneys scurrying for cover beneath their counsel tables.[56]

Pierce continued to press the habeas corpus and bail issues in similar motions naming other defendants, but Judge Jones found that no new evidence had been presented since the previous hearings to warrant release of the prisoners.[57] The judge's intransigence stimulated whispered criticism among the five newsmen covering the proceedings, and word reached the judge that he was about to be "skinned" in the press. This rumor was coupled to a report that

[53] *Nashville Tennessean,* November 7, 1908, p. 1.

[54] *Ibid.,* p. 8.

[55] *Nashville Banner,* November 7, 1908, p. 2; *Nashville American,* November 7, 1908, p. 1.

[56] *Nashville Banner,* November 7, 1908, p. 2; personal interview on October 21, 1956, with Tom Southworth in Union City. Hereinafter cited as "Southworth interview."

[57] *Nashville Tennessean,* November 11, 1908, p. 3.

Pierce intended to release a statement critical of the judge's decisions. Jones warned the correspondents not to publish anything that reflected on the court's actions or judgement, and furthermore, if any correspondent attempted to "skin" him, he would be jailed for contempt.[58] No such "skinnings" appeared in print.

Thwarted in Union City, Rice Pierce searched for a more favorable reception in the circuit court of Judge Thomas E. Matthews in Nashville. Petitions similar to those filed with Judge Jones were presented on behalf of the nine prisoners held in Davidson County Jail. There was one difference. In this instance the defense agreed to settle on reasonable bail for the defendants rather than to argue first for their outright release, as had been done in Union City. Still Pierce intended to question the governor's right to call out the militia before pursuing the matter of bail. Arguments for both sides were substantially the same as those advanced in Union City. In his decision, however, Judge Matthews arrived at a radically different conclusion. The arrest of the suspects was "irregular," he said, "because the General Assembly had not declared that public safety demanded activation of the militia." But, he admitted, "conditions in Obion County were extraordinary, the necessity of these conditions were great and pressing, and everyone concerned acted honestly, in good faith and with no motives other than to promote the general welfare of society and the best interests of the state." [59]

Still, in Judge Matthews' view, the governor had acted unconstitutionally, and the prisoners were entitled to immediate release. However, as they had agreed to accept bail, he would hold them in custody until that question had been resolved. The lawyers were given two weeks (to December 2) to prepare their briefs. Pierce had won at least a partial victory, one which brought tears to the eyes of several of the prisoners, the first sign of emotion since their arrests.[60]

The prosecution faced precisely the same dilemma on the bond matter as had bedeviled it in Union City. Either it had to produce evidence supporting capital charges against the suspects or agree to bond. The former was unwelcome, the latter was impossible.[61] Still

---

58 *Ibid.; Nashville American,* November 11, 1908, p. 1.

59 *Chattanooga Daily Times,* November 19, 1908, p. 1.

60 *Nashville American,* November 19, 1908, p. 1.

61 *Chattanooga Daily Times,* November 19, 1908, p. 1.

the State's attorneys were not short on strategy. They knew that by the first week in December a legally constituted grand jury would return capital crime indictments against a number of defendants, who then could not be bonded under state law. If the suspects in Nashville could be held in custody until that time, the bond issue would become moot. It was taken for granted that Judge Matthews would order bond set for the prisoners in Nashville. Such bond would have to be executed in Obion County, where the alleged crimes had been committed. When the bonds were set, the prosecution planned to serve the suspects immediately with warrants charging them with capital night riding crimes. The warrants were to be based on indictments voted by the current, illegally constituted grand jury. But this flaw would be corrected a few days later with new indictments issued by the properly seated grand jurors. To refute the defense contention that the suspects had not yet been charged with a crime, the State had Obion County authorities swear out warrants that charged each Nashville defendant with a capital offense. These were read by a jailer to the prisoners in their cells. The prosecution, however, never intended to support these warrants with meaningful evidence in its arguments before Judge Matthews.[62] Finally, as insurance against possible failure of the State's plan, Sheriff Haynes stood by in Nashville with warrants charging the nine with night riding in Lake County. Had their attorneys solved the legal labyrinth designed to hold the prisoners in Obion County, the suspects would have been subjected to Lake County justice,[63] a prospect which pleased neither the Riders nor their lawyers.

While awaiting a determination in Judge Matthews' court, one of the prisoners, Tom Wilson, died of congestive chills. A poor man, forty-six years old, with a wife and six children, he had earned his living by farming a portion of his brother's farm.[64] Neighbors noticed with pity that during her husband's imprisonment, Mrs. Wilson had been forced to cut firewood and her young boys to do their father's chores. When the prisoner died, the lake community be-

[62] *Ibid.,* December 4, 1908, p. 1; *Nashville Tennessean,* December 4, 1908, p. 1.

[63] *Nashville Banner,* November 16, 1908, p. 1.

[64] *Ibid.,* November 19, 1908, p. 11; *Chattanooga Daily Times,* November 21, 1908, p. 2; and *McNairy County Independent,* November 27, 1908, p. 3.

came more angered than grieved, and the State feared a resurgence of night rider violence. Such an outburst did not occur, but Wilson's death gave impetus to already prevalent rumors that the prisoners were being poorly treated in Nashville, that they were cramped together, with little room in which to exercise and breathe decent air—important losses to rural people. As Reelfoot's natives grew more restless, the State pressed even harder to bring its night riding cases to trial.[65]

Judge Matthews neither disappointed the defense nor surprised the prosecution. On December 2, he declared that the State had made nothing more than unsubstantiated accusations against the defendants, and "a mere accusation, however forward, should not so far destroy the presumption of innocence as to deprive the accused of bail . . ." [66] Then, criticizing the State's entire procedure against the Night Riders, he said, ". . . I am bound to declare that legal forms and high politics of constitutional procedure were not observed either in the original capture or in the detention of the prisoners." [67] Moreover, the service of warrants on the prisoners while the question of bail was pending amounted to contempt of court. However, the contempt was ruled an "honest mistake" and no citations followed.[68] The prisoners should be freed, continued the judge, but because of the agreement among counsel, bail would be set at $10,000 for four of the men, and $5,000 for the others. The cases were then referred back to Obion County, where bond would be made.

As the prisoners prepared to embark by train for Union City, one of their members, Jesse Carter, fell ill with malaria and remained in custody of medical personnel at the Nashville jail.[69] The other seven departed Nashville on December 4, and when they arrived at Union City they were welcomed by a cheering crowd of their kinsmen. "It was as if seven heroes who had performed some gallant deed, done their countrymen some great service or won fame and distinction in some way other than being arrested and charged with one of the

---

[65] *Chattanooga Daily Times,* November 21, 1908, p. 2.

[66] *Nashville Tennessean,* December 4, 1908, p. 1.

[67] *Ibid.,* p. 3.

[68] *Ibid.; Chattanooga Daily Times,* December 3, 1908, p. 1.

[69] *Nashville American,* December 4, 1908, p. 10; *Nashville Tennessean,* December 4, 1908, p. 1.

most brutal and bloody crimes that has ever been recorded, were entering the city." [70] Pierce confidently announced to the gathering of hundreds that the seven soon would be released on bond to rejoin their families. What Pierce did not realize was that the Obion Grand Jury had just voted hurried indictments against each defendant, charging them not with Rankin's murder, but with felonious assault while masked at night, a violation of the Ku Klux Klan Act and punishable by death.[71] The following day, December 5, when Tom Johnson and Elijah Cloar made bond, they were immediately served with the new warrants charging them with the unbailable offense. Then they were rearrested.[72] Pierce recognized the futility of pursuing the matter of bail any further with these defendants.[73] No arguments he could produce were going to alter the determination of Judge Jones to retain the prisoners in custody until they could be tried.

Governor Patterson, meanwhile, had been easily re-elected over George N. Tillman.[74] Newspapers, such as the *Chattanooga Daily Times,* editorialized, "The most promising feature of his [Patterson's] administration, shown as a result of the night-rider's outbreak in West Tennessee, is that he has started out to see that the law is enforced . . ." [75] This comment was more prod than praise, and Governor Patterson was determined to sustain the image and political dividends he had accrued by his actions following Rankin's death. He therefore ordered the prosecution into high gear. The State began by sifting through its heavy volume of evidence, assessing its credibility and weighing it against the more than 100 suspects in custody in order to determine against whom it should ask the grand jury to return indictments for Rankin's murder. Concerning the defense, the *Nashville Tennessean* noted that Rice Pierce "up to the present, has played his hand in full consciousness of his friendship for Governor Patterson and the party he represented. Now with the election over, Pierce may be expected to forget the friendship and

[70] *The Commercial Appeal,* December 5, 1908, p. 1.
[71] *Nashville Banner,* December 4, 1908, p. 1.
[72] *Nashville American,* December 6, 1908, p. 3.
[73] *Chattanooga Sunday Times,* December 6, 1908, p. 1.
[74] *Chattanooga Daily Times,* November 4, 1908, p. 1.
[75] *Ibid.,* p. 4.

fight for his clients." [76] That is precisely what Pierce intended to do. Regardless of whom the grand jury indicted, it was known that the defense would consist of alibis, supported by character witnesses, and a relentless attack upon the State's case, particularly the testimony of Riders who had turned state's evidence.

Once safely in office for a second term, Governor Patterson also attempted to explain to his critics why his responses to night riding in Middle Tennessee and at Reelfoot Lake had been divergent. In sharp contrast to his enthusiastic campaign to rid the lake of the Riders, the governor had done nothing to quell the night riding in Montgomery County (Clarksville) when the tobacco war movement in southern Kentucky had spilled over the stateline into north-central Tennessee. His critics charged political expediency inhibited the governor's desire to end the crime wave in Montgomery. Patterson, however, insisted, "Conditions are different there [Montgomery]. Both the sheriff and judge of the court there requested that I should not call out the troops, protesting that civil authorities could handle the situation." [77] Turning to the Reelfoot case, Patterson noted that both the Obion sheriff and the circuit judge of the district had requested the assistance of the militia. Therefore, he had complied. [78]

One may be reasonably certain that Governor Patterson balked in the Montgomery County situation for political reasons. In that county, the judge and sheriff apparently were not unfriendly to the night riding element and therefore invited no state interference. In turn, the governor needed these county officials for political support. He could not risk the possibility of losing Montgomery County support scant months before the election; therefore, he declined to intervene in that county's night riding problems.

Local conditions differed in West Tennessee. There local officials demanded the vigorous prosecution of Rankin's murderers and an end to night riding at Reelfoot Lake. Had the governor not summoned the militia, he would have faced serious political repercussions throughout the western portion, if not all, of his state.

Governor Patterson saw state intervention in local night riding affairs as a political risk, especially in an election year. Before

76 *Nashville Tennessean,* November 4, 1908, p. 1.
77 *Nashville Banner,* November 13, 1908, p. 2.
78 *Ibid.*

Rankin's death, Lake County authorities had petitioned his assistance against Reelfoot's Riders but had been ignored. It took a tragedy and the pressure of an outraged public to pry the governor off his political middleground. The irony is that, once moved to act, he unwittingly became the recipient of an enormous political bonus.

Probing newsmen also questioned the governor about his procedure against Reelfoot's clan. Had the Obion County Sheriff requested the aid of the state militia, as required by Tennessee law? Governor Patterson assured the correspondents that he had. But Sheriff Easterwood had difficulty remembering whether or not he had in fact requested the troops. First he said that he had not. Then on November 6 he had told the press that he remembered signing a statement on the previous October 25 asking the governor to send in the militia.[79] Later Easterwood reverted to his original position.[80]

What actually occurred is difficult to determine. Easterwood had never been anxious to attack the night rider problem. Therefore, it seems unlikely that he would have requested state troops even after Rankin's murder. What probably occurred is this: Patterson called out the state guard immediately upon learning of Rankin's murder. Some time later, but well after the soldiers had entrained for Reelfoot, Patterson sought to fulfill the legal requirement which governed the sending of troops to a specific county. He then telephoned Easterwood and told him to request the militia. In sum total, this was simply another example of the way in which the State leapfrogged legal technicalities in its anxiety to proceed with the prosecution.

Governor Patterson had met with prosecuting attorneys and his military advisors on November 12 in Union City to begin consolidation of the State's case. Those implicated by strong evidence would be held. Weak cases would be dismissed, and bail permitted for a middle group against whom reasonable proof had been developed.[81] Forty prisoners considered prime suspects were ordered transferred to Union City to join the fourteen already there, plus the eight from Nashville.[82] Confederate Veterans Hall across the main square from the courthouse was rented as a barracks for soldiers,

---

[79] *Ibid.*, November 9, 1908, p. 8.
[80] Easterwood interview.
[81] *Nashville Banner*, November 13, 1908, p. 1.
[82] *Nashville American*, November 14, 1908, p. 2.

prisoners, and reporters.[83] The garrison at Nemo was to be broken up, but forty militiamen would remain at the lake under Captain C. B. Rogan, a retired army officer, for continuing patrol duty. Colonel Tatom eased his "shoot to kill" edict. Now soldiers were to shout "Halt!" three times before firing, and the first shot was to be aimed over the head of the suspect. After that, militiamen could shoot at the suspect.[84]

Captain Ben Capell was to command a detachment of fifty soldiers from the Memphis contingent needed to escort the prisoners from Nemo to Union City and then garrison the city pending the trial.[85] Lake County possemen volunteered to guard the prisoners during the twenty mile trip to Union City, but Colonel Tatom declined the offer, saying, "I'm afraid you'd never get there with them," to which Captain F. W. Shaw responded, "Well, we'd save the State a little money." [86] The remaining soldiers were to be released from duty and sent home.

There were other reasons for evacuating the prisoners from Camp Nemo. Continuing reports that the suspects had been mistreated had created dangerous tensions in the district—tensions which threatened to prejudice potential jurors against the state. It was said that the soldiers cursed the prisoners and for fun jabbed them with bayonets; that they had forced suspects to live on meager food and in filthy tents with no blankets; that the natives were "treated like valueless dogs or hogs not intended for fattening." [87] The *Nashville Tennessean* investigated these reports and found them false.[88] In a statement to the press, Colonel Tatom discounted rumors that families of prisoners were starving: "Under positive instructions of Governor Patterson, we are caring for not only the families of the prisoners who are not in a position to care for themselves, but all others who come to us seeking aid or protection. These families who are reported to be in destitute circumstances are daily bringing pies and

83 *Ibid.*, November 6, 1908, p. 3.

84 *Chattanooga Daily Times*, November 3, 1908, p. 4.

85 *Nashville Banner*, November 13, 1908, p. 4; *Nashville American*, November 15, 1908, p. 5.

86 *Nashville American*, October 30, 1908, p. 9.

87 *Nashville Tennessean*, November 9, 1908, p. 5.

88 *Ibid.*

cakes and other delicacies to the prisoners, such as the soldiers would be glad to get." [89]

Actually, conditions appear to have been tolerable, and the prisoners themselves had few complaints. Reports of mistreatment in the main were the product of a deliberate psychological campaign conducted by a Baptist preacher on behalf of the defense.[90]

The Reverend Richard R. Marshall, pastor of the First Baptist Church in Kankakee, Illinois, had returned to the Reelfoot region to post bail for his brother, Ed Marshall; he remained to inaugurate a "moral persuasion" movement to prejudice prospective jurors, if not to free the prisoners. Petitions demanding a speedy and fair trial were circulated in an attempt to unify the region behind the "oppressed" suspects. Families were said to be in want. There was unattended sickness at home. Land lay fallow and businesses were failing.[91]

The State tried to counter the propaganda with an attentive attitude toward the prisoners and their families.[92] However, its pacification program was upset when newspapers exposed conditions surrounding the untimely death of Jesse Carter, the prisoner with malaria who had been retained in Nashville. While tossing in pain, Carter had been manacled with a heavy chain to his bed and kept under constant guard by a deputy sheriff. Only when the thirty-four-year-old bachelor was delirious and near death were the padlock and chain removed. Such callousness undoubtedly created indignation in the minds of many citizens, even those most anxious to eliminate night riding,[93] and a growing revulsion for state authority at times erupted into violence.

There had been sporadic incidents between the militia and Night Riders, or purported Riders, since Camp Nemo had been established. However, following the November reduction of the camp's contingent to forty men, the unidentified forces harassing the soldiers

[89] *The Commercial Appeal,* November 12, 1908, p. 2.

[90] *Nashville Tennessean,* November 13, 1908, p. 3.

[91] *Ibid.; Atlanta Constitution,* November 10, 1908, p. 9; and *Nashville Banner,* November 9, 1908, p. 8.

[92] Capell interview.

[93] *Nashville Tennessean,* November 21, 1908, p. 6; *Carroll County Democrat* (Huntingdon, Tenn.), December 18, 1908, p. 4; and *The Commercial Appeal,* December 5, 1908, p. 3.

became bolder. Captain Rogan had renamed the post Fort Rankin and had ordered the construction of permanent barracks. Much of the lumber needed by the military was furnished by Gleason's Sawmill, which had suspended business the previous spring when threatened by "Night Riders," who in actuality may have been business competitors masquerading as clansmen. Under the protection of the military, the mill had resumed operation in mid-November, and when unknown parties threatened arson, a detachment of soldiers was stationed at the plant. One night an exchange of rifle fire erupted between the sentries and unseen assailants, and a soldier was wounded in the hand. A search of the surrounding cornfields the following morning, however, revealed no trace of the intruders.[94] Were the interlopers Night Riders? Perhaps. The military acknowledged that they also could have been either adventurers or commercial rivals of the Gleasons.[95]

The most serious difficulty encountered by the military establishment involved a threatened mutiny within its own ranks. The issue was pay. The 1887 legislature had provided that national guardsmen on active duty would receive pay equal to that of respective U. S. Army ranks. But for those who served less than thirty days on active duty, a special state militia scale had been provided.[96] There was a substantial difference in daily pay, especially for officers, between the two systems. Colonels received $11.11 a day under the army scale and $3.50 by state standards; for majors the pay was $8.33 against $3; captains, $6.66 against $3; and lieutenants, $4.75 against $2. Service under the state schedule provided non-commissioned staff officers and sergeants with $1 a day, regular sergeants and corporals, eighty cents, and privates, fifty cents, none of them far below regular army rates.[97]

When Governor Patterson announced that troops which had not completed thirty days service would receive the lower state pay, of-

[94] *Chattanooga Sunday Times,* November 29, 1908, p. 1; *Nashville Banner,* November 28, 1908, p. 1.

[95] Capell interview.

[96] *Chattanooga Daily Times,* November 17, 1908, p. 10.

[97] *Nashville Tennessean,* November 15, 1908, p. 1; *Nashville Banner,* November 16, 1908, p. 7.

ficers at Nemo held an "indignation" meeting at which they agreed
to accept the state scale, but under protest. The simmering protest
soon erupted in anger. Soldiers hanged and burned in effigy Harvey
Alexander, who directed military pay affairs from the statehouse in
Nashville. Officers threatened to quit their units, and for a time it
appeared that the entire militia would disband itself and head for
home.[98]

Governor Patterson found himself in a difficult position. Public
opinion, including that of prominent friends such as Attorney General
Caldwell, agreed that the soldiers had well earned the higher
pay. Yet he could hardly tolerate mutiny among the men of whom
he was commander-in-chief. Patterson arrived at a compromise.
Captain Phillips, who operated the military commissary in Union
City, where the militia was paid, received orders from Colonel Alexander:
"The governor orders you to pay state pay. If authority can
be found, additional payment will be made later." [99] Then it was
quietly conceded that the soldiers returning to their home bases
would be technically retained on active status until the thirty-day
requirement had been fulfilled.[100] As to the effigy incident, Patterson
thought the offenders should be disciplined, but because of their
splendid record in the field against the Riders, he decided against
further investigation.[101]

Pierce made several more unsuccessful attempts to win bail for
suspects not yet indicted. Fred Pinion, said to be a leader of the
Riders, was brought from his cell in Dyersburg to seek bond, but
Judge Jones reiterated that bail would not be considered while the
grand jury continued in session.[102] One suspect, John Ratliff, offered
to make a $200,000 bond so that he might tend to critical
matters at his general store near Clayton. He faced bankruptcy, he
said, if he could not get home before local farmers sold their cotton
crops and spent their proceeds elsewhere than with him. When his
request for bail was rejected, Ratliff suggested that the foreman of

[98] *Nashville Banner*, November 16, 1908, p. 7.
[99] *Nashville Tennessean*, November 15, 1908, p. 1.
[100] *Ibid.*, November 14, 1908, p. 1.
[101] *Nashville Banner*, December 21, 1908, p. 2.
[102] *Nashville American*, November 23, 1908, p. 10.

the grand jury accompany him to his store. After business was settled, they would return together. The prosecution, however, refused to yield in his case.[103]

As for the prisoners who had turned state's evidence, they received most careful attention from the State. Governor Patterson often personally visited them, assuring himself of both their welfare and their willingness to testify against their former comrades.[104]

For Thanksgiving, businessmen contributed the money with which ladies of the city purchased and prepared turkeys, hams, cakes, custards, pies, and salads to be served to defendant and soldier without discrimination.[105] "The long tables [in the barracks] were resplendent in white damask and gleamed with cut glass and silver. All of the ladies brought their silver, china, glassware and drapery from their homes . . ."[106] The scene resembled a festive community get-together rather than an impending murder trial.

In the military barracks which housed both the soldiers and suspects a similar aura of friendship prevailed. In the evenings the militiamen and prisoners often sang together. "Nearer My God to Thee" and "Old-Time Religion" were their favorites, "all sung with great muscular power and full of enjoyment, to say nothing of the melody."[107]

However, the specter of the trial was not allowed to fade. Newspapers, which poorly understood and often misinterpreted the pretrial procedures, accused attorneys of deliberate delay. "The situation in Obion County is such that a resort to the trickeries of the law by pettifogging lawyers should not be tolerated . . . ," insisted the *Carroll County Democrat*.[108] Despite such impatience, neither side counseled delay, and the cases moved steadily toward trial.[109]

[103] *Nashville Banner*, November 17, 1908, p. 9.

[104] *Nashville American*, November 15, 1908, p. 5.

[105] *Ibid.*, November 27, 1908, p. 2; *Nashville Banner*, November 23, 1908, p. 1.

[106] *The Commercial Appeal*, November 27, 1908, p. 3.

[107] *Chattanooga Daily Times*, November 21, 1908, p. 2.

[108] *Carroll County Democrat*, November 6, 1908, p. 4.

[109] Miles interview.

CHAPTER 6

THE TRIAL: EVIDENCE AND ALIBIS

IT WAS AN anxious Union City that prepared itself for the Night Rider trials in December, 1908. More than 100 suspects had been arrested, and the State considered evidence against sixty-three of them sufficient to warrant their retention in the prisoners' barracks. But how many Night Riders had not yet been apprehended? It was rumored that a nucleus of the band still roamed at liberty and that Union City was liable to attack at any moment.

"The soldiers were sleeping under arms in their quarters . . . The crash of a rifle aroused everyone . . . In less than two minutes every soldier was at his post. The black muzzles of rifles peered from every window in the building." [1] In this instance, the alarm was false. A soldier had accidentally fired his "unloaded" rifle while cleaning it.[2] But the lesson was plain: the militia was nervously alert, expecting the worst from the Night Riders.

[1] *The Commercial Appeal,* November 23, 1908, p. 1.
[2] James interview.

Strange signaling with red lights reported in one neighborhood proved to be only danger lamps placed by laborers on a sewer excavation.[3] Four men were arrested as Night Riders when found trespassing in a stable, but they were detained only a few minutes when authorities discovered that they were young drunks rather than Riders attempting to steal new mounts.[4]

The Riders had considered attacking Union City the past September in order to "get" Attorney General Caldwell and Circuit Judge Jones, but the two officials had unexpectedly left town to hold special court in Camden, and the clansmen had contented themselves by forwarding them threatening letters.[5]

Governor Patterson assured the citizenry: "As long as the midnight bands of marauders continue to operate in this country, threatening people by their vile letters and warnings, I'll keep every man in the state under arms for a year or more if necessary [until] it [night riding] is put down and stopped." [6] Encouraging words from the governor, but the question remained, could the militia contain the remaining Night Riders? Many feared not.

Major legal interest in the Night Rider cases now centered on the selection of the new special grand jury scheduled to meet December 7. By law, Judge Jones was to appoint three justices from Obion County who within ten days would prepare a list of thirty-five prospective jurors for the special term. The sheriff would then summon the veniremen, and a jury of thirteen would be chosen from among them for the special term.[7]

Judge Jones, however, in his propensity for eliminating harassing technicalities which impeded progress toward trial, routinely reappointed all but two members of the original jury to the new term. Of those two, one was ill and the other out of the city, so they were replaced.[8] The introduction of evidence before the new group was perfunctory. Written statements given by witnesses such as R. Z. Taylor, P. C. Ward, Ed Powell, and Frank Fehringer were simply

3 *The Commercial Appeal,* November 26, 1908, p. 2.

4 *Ibid.*

5 *Ibid.,* November 8, 1908, p. 2.

6 *Ibid.,* November 13, 1908, p. 1.

7 *Nashville Banner,* December 9, 1908, p. 1.

8 *Nashville Tennessean,* December 8, 1908, p. 2.

read to the new jury and again signed by the witnesses,[9] and on December 8 the jury returned indictments charging eight men with the murder of Rankin. The defendants included Sam Applewhite, Garrett Johnson, Arthur Cloar, Bob Huffman, Fred Pinion, Roy Ransom, Bud Morris, and Tid Burton.[10] At their arraignment the following day, all pleaded not guilty.[11] They displayed no emotion with the exception of Fred Pinion who for the first time since his arrest was united with his family—his aged mother, wife, and several small children, the youngest being a girl of about three years old—"and as he took a seat beside his wife and took his baby girl in his arms, he could not restrain himself any longer, and he broke down and wept. The little girl was the only member of the family that was not in tears during the entire time that he was allowed to talk to his wife." [12]

Rice Pierce futilely protested that Judge Jones had erred in designating the members of the grand jury by himself; therefore, Rice contended, the indictments returned by the jury were invalid.[13] The judge, however, remained adamant and set the trial for December 14.[14]

The second grand jury continued to consider the same evidence that had been presented to the first, and within a few days had voted a total of 142 indictments, thirteen more than the first jury.[15] The charges, overlapping as to defendants, alleged murder and various night riding violations of the Ku Klux Klan Act, including felonious assault while in disguise and the burning of Burdick's docks.[16] Conviction under the act carried a minimum sentence of twenty years.

Public speculation now turned to selection of the trial jury. "The question has been asked a thousand times," wrote the *Dresden Enter-*

[9] *Chattanooga Daily Times,* December 8, 1908, p. 1.

[10] *Nashville Banner,* December 9, 1908, p. 2.

[11] Tennessee, Circuit Court, "Minute Book J," in Records of the Circuit Court (in Obion County Courthouse, Union City, Tenn.), December 10, 1908, p. 82.

[12] *The Commercial Appeal,* December 11, 1908, p. 3.

[13] *Nashville Tennessean,* December 10, 1908, p. 1; *Nashville Banner,* December 9, 1908, p. 1.

[14] *Nashville Banner,* December 10, 1908, p. 1.

[15] *Nashville Tennessean,* December 8, 1908, p. 2, and December 13, 1908, p. 2.

[16] *Chattanooga Daily Times,* December 12, 1908, p. 1.

prise, "can a jury be secured in Obion County with sufficient courage and backbone to convict." [17] Neither the prosecution nor the defense thought that it could, and they had ample precedent to support their contention. At this stage, however, the State could not concern itself with the problem of possible convictions; the prosecution feared that it might not even be able to qualify a jury to try the case. Details of the Night Rider rebellion had been in the news for weeks. Had not all prospective jurors in Obion, where the case, by law, had to be tried, already formed an opinion as to the guilt or innocence of the defendants? If so, they could not serve on the jury, and this would not have been the first time that an Obion Night Rider case had failed to reach trial because of the inability to select a qualified jury. Clearly local conditions favored the defense, but the prosecution had devised a bold strategy with which it hoped to counteract the unfavorable situation. In this regard, the State began by asking Judge Jones to select the jury venire personally, rather than having it chosen at random as was customary. [18]

Legally, Judge Jones had authority to pick the jury panel in extraordinary cases. Otherwise, the sheriff called prospective jurors for examination. The defense argued that the Night Rider cases did not constitute an extraordinary situation, but Judge Jones ruled otherwise—an opinion for which he can hardly be faulted. A venire of 300 men would be selected for jury service, announced the judge, and those who deliberately attempted to disqualify themselves would be held in contempt of court. [19]

The *Fayette Falcon* was among several newspapers that applauded the decision of the judge: "The action of Judge Jones . . . in naming his venire of jurymen . . . while unusual, shows the power of the state and the determination of the court to use every effort to uphold the arm of the law." [20]

Sheriff Easterwood and his deputies worked throughout the night to summon the veniremen. When court convened the next day, De-

17 *Dresden Enterprise,* December 18, 1908, p. 2.

18 *Chattanooga Daily Times,* December 11, 1908, p. 1; *Atlanta Journal,* December 14, 1908, p. 1.

19 *Nashville Tennessean,* December 15, 1908, p. 1; *Nashville Banner,* December 15, 1908, pp. 2 and 14; *Chattanooga Daily Times,* December 15, 1908, p. 1.

20 *Fayette Falcon* (Fayetteville, Tenn.), December 18, 1908, p. 4.

cember 16, he had 252 prospective jurors in court. Judge Jones stated that the defense would be allowed twenty-four peremptory challenges for each defendant, or a total of 192, while the State would have six per defendant, or forty-eight in all.[21]

In the first day's work only two men out of fifty-three examined were accepted by both sides for jury service. Judge Jones declared twenty-four incompetent, usually because they admitted having set opinions. The defense employed twenty-six peremptory challenges in dismissing veniremen without debate and the State only one.[22] At that rate of attrition, it appeared that the panel would be exhausted before a jury could be seated. The State, however, had prepared for this contingency. Admittedly, it was to be a desperate gamble, an unprecedented maneuver, but if it could withstand the legal test, it might produce a jury willing to convict the defendants.

As jury selection continued the next day, the State immediately challenged the first selected juror, W. H. Russell, labeling him the father of an alleged Night Rider who had been sworn into the band by a defendant now on trial. (The son had turned State's evidence.) Russell admitted being the father of Charles Russell but swore he did not know that his son was a suspected Rider. Judge Jones ruled the father-son relationship constituted sufficient cause to excuse Russell from jury duty.[23]

Then, when the defense exercised its first peremptory challenge of the day, Assistant Attorney General Major Hal Holmes issued a sharp objection. He alleged that the defense had exhausted its allotment of peremptory challenges the preceding day. A murmur of surprise circulated in the courtroom. Pierce frowned. Holmes went on to explain the State's position. The defense, by law, he said, was allowed a total of twenty-four challenges for *each* defendant, or a total of 192, which the Court had allowed; however, the prosecution

[21] *Nashville Banner,* December 16, 1908, p. 1. There is no limit to the number of challenges for reasonable cause, but when using a peremptory challenge, counsel need not prove cause, and the challenged person is dismissed without debate. The number of peremptory challenges allowed for various types of cases is set by state law.

[22] *The Commercial Appeal,* December 17, 1908, p. 1; *Nashville Tennessean,* December 17, 1908, p. 1.

[23] *The Commercial Appeal,* December 17, 1908, p. 1; *Chattanooga Daily Times,* December 18, 1908, p. 1.

believed it implicit in the law that each challenge be made in the name of a specific defendant. The defense had not done this; therefore, it must be assumed that it had challenged collectively for all defendants. Under those circumstances, it was entitled to only twenty-four challenges as if only one defendant were on trial. As the defense had spent twenty-six of its challenges the previous day, its right to further peremptory challenges had been expended.[24]

Caught off balance, Pierce argued vehemently against the prosecution's unexpected tactics. Even when Judge Jones sustained the State's claim, Pierce continued to object. This objection led the judge to observe: "The court has been very patient and lenient thus far, but unless Mr. Pierce ceases from his attempts to violate the court's ruling, the court will exercise its right to remove Mr. Pierce from the case and appoint other counsel to conduct the examination [of prospective jurors]." That calmed the chief counsel for the defense.[25]

Selection of the remaining eleven jurors proceeded without incident. Each side could still have challenged for cause, but only the State had remaining peremptory challenges, none of which were used. When the jury box was filled, half of its members were from Union City proper, where Obion citizens were most antagonistic toward the Night Riders. None of the other six came from the lake district. Seven were farmers, and the other five included a grocer, bookkeeper, salesman, manufacturer, and grain dealer.[26]

Lawyers attending the hearing, some of them among the most prominent members of the Tennessee bar, found the peremptory challenge decision of Judge Jones to be "sweeping" and "of national importance." They said that they did not know of a single case in the history of United States' jurisprudence where the same question had been raised and decided.[27]

Faced by the improbability of seating a trial jury, the State had gambled and presumably had won. Judge Swiggart, among the most

[24] *The Commercial Appeal,* December 18, 1908, p. 1.

[25] *Chattanooga Daily Times,* December 18, 1908, p. 1; *Atlanta Constitution,* December 18, 1908, p. 5.

[26] *Chattanooga Daily Times,* December 18, 1908, p. 1; *Nashville Tennessean,* December 18, 1908, p. 5.

[27] *Nashville Tennessean,* December 18, 1908, p. 1; Miles interview.

able of the prosecutors, said that the "question was a close and nice point of law." While the State did not welcome any error in the record, it had decided after careful deliberation that it would take its chances with the matter in a higher court.[28] The State realized that any convictions would be appealed, and the peremptory challenge question might well decide that appeal. Also the prosecution recognized that a reversal of any conviction would be tantamount to freedom for the defendants. Only the unrealistic failed to understand the unlikelihood of ever being able to secure a second jury to retry the Rankin murder case.[29] The peremptory challenge issue was a thin thread on which to hang a nationally prominent murder case, but for the prosecution it seemed to provide the only chance for success.

Subpoenas for 110 state and 110 defense witnesses had been served by Sheriff Easterwood, but as the trial opened on December 17 only seventy-four were sworn in for the State and sixty-seven for the defense.[30] The summoning of more than 100 witnesses for each side had been more a psychological than a practical measure, and few of the witnesses believed important to their respective cases failed to appear at the swearing-in. Many of those sworn were never called to testify.[31]

Spectators packed the courtroom as the testimony began, filling the aisles as well as the stairs and corridors leading to the chamber. The majority consisted of Union City townspeople. Few lake residents were evident.[32] Both uniformed militiamen and sheriff's deputies patrolled the scene.[33]

Judge Jones expressly prohibited newsmen from directly quoting the testimony of witnesses. Verbatim reports, he said, would only further prejudice potential jurors in Obion County and complicate jury selection in future night riding trials. The judge placed the correspondents on their honor to comply and threatened censorship

[28] *Nashville Banner,* December 17, 1908, p. 1.

[29] Miles interview.

[30] *Chattanooga Daily Times,* December 16, 1908, p. 1; *Nashville Banner,* December 18, 1908, p. 1.

[31] Miles interview.

[32] *Chattanooga Daily Times,* December 19, 1908, p. 1.

[33] Capell interview.

if they did not.[34] The reporters agreed to, then ignored, the judge's request. Most of the important testimony was directly reported in print, and Jones took no reprisals. Preachers were more obedient to the judge's plea that the case not be discussed from the pulpit.[35]

Events leading to the murder of Quentin Rankin were related in the testimony of James F. Carpenter and Seid Waddell, who had made the arrangements which led the attorneys to their fate at Walnut Log.[36] Ed Powell told how he was dragged from bed and made to accompany the Riders to Ward's hotel and the murder scene. He identified Fehringer as a member of the lynch mob, Garrett Johnson as its leader, and Roy Ransom as a man in a white mask.[37]

> When Powell boldly announced that Garrett Johnson was the leader of the band and minutely described the disguise which he wore: told of how he carried a heavy black snake whip draped fantastically about his neck: told of how he had been called from the head of the procession of death back to where Powell marched under heavy guard to administer the oath of fealty, Garrett Johnson blanched and quailed as his eyes met the fearless ones of his accuser. He trembled in his seat and went ghost white . . ." [38]

The following day Colonel R. Z. Taylor, composed in emotion and soldierly in appearance, took the stand to recount the ordeal that he and Rankin had experienced at the hands of the masked assassins followed by his own miraculous escape from death. When Taylor had arrived at his hometown of Trenton following the tragedy, he had been hailed as a hero and carried through town on the shoulders of friends. "Be careful," he had told them, "I'm still mighty tender." [39] At the trial Taylor was neither tender of body nor of will. He was determined that Rankin's murderers and his own tormentors should hang.[40] Taylor's shortcoming as a prosecution witness lay in his inability to identify any of the Riders at the murder scene. In

---

[34] *Chattanooga Daily Times,* December 19, 1908, p. 1; *Nashville Banner,* December 21, 1908, p. 6.

[35] Miles interview.

[36] *Nashville Banner,* December 18, 1908, p. 11; *Chattanooga Daily Times,* December 19, 1908, p. 3.

[37] *Chattanooga Daily Times,* December 19, 1908, p. 3.

[38] *The Commercial Appeal,* December 19, 1908, p. 1.

[39] *St. Louis Post-Dispatch,* December 19, 1908, p. 1; *McNairy County Independent,* October 30, 1908, p. 2.

[40] Taylor interview.

fact, Rice Pierce asked him only one question in cross-examination: "Did you recognize any of the Riders positively the night of the crime?" Taylor replied, "I did not." [41] The former Confederate soldier testified during re-examination that he had been struck twice at the murder site by a man who had whiskers or wore a mask that resembled whiskers. Since that time Taylor said he had seen a man of similar appearance.

"Who?" inquired Caldwell.

"Garrett Johnson," responded the witness.[42] But this was weak identification.

Regardless of the content of his testimony, Taylor made a dramatic witness whose presence alone must have influenced the jury. "At times his emotions mastered him, and once he half turned, dropped his head into his hands and sobbed audibly as the scenes of that awful night passed again before his eyes." [43] Although he could not pinpoint Rankin's murderers, Taylor could describe their general appearance, intentions and methods, all of which were crucial to the State's basic theory that Rankin's death constituted only one brutal incident in a monstrous conspiracy to control the Reelfoot region.

With the testimony of Charles H. Russell, a Rider who had turned state's evidence, the State began to link specific defendants to the charges. Russell stated that Arthur Cloar induced him to join the Riders. The defense objected that such testimony did not concern the murder of Rankin, but the State reiterated its conspiracy thesis, and the court sustained its position.[44]

The witness most vital to the prosecution was Frank Fehringer, and his performance on the stand did not disappoint the State.

> Surrounded by a detail of six soldiers with loaded rifles and revolver holsters open, Frank Fehringer . . . was brought into the courtroom . . . to testify against his former associates of the mask. At the courtroom door, the soldiers with rifles halted. Four other soldiers armed with revolvers took charge. Four armed deputies cleared a way through the crowd in the aisles, and Fehringer was led to the stand. The soldiers sat down inside the railing facing the throng. Other deputies, armed heav-

41 *Atlanta Journal*, December 19, 1908, p. 2.
42 *The Sun*, December 20, 1908, p. 7.
43 *St. Louis Post-Dispatch*, December 19, 1908, p. 2.
44 *Atlanta Journal*, December 19, 1908, p. 2.

ily, scattered quietly through the room. It was a tense moment. The witness, a slight man [5'8" tall and 150 pounds], was composed but pale. He crossed his legs nonchalantly and tossed his broad-brimmed hat on the toe of his boot.[45]

Fehringer repeated the oath, passwords, and other supposed secrets of the Riders, and he placed Garrett Johnson, Bob Huffman, Bud Morris, and Sam Applewhite at the murder scene.[46] Under three hours of cross-examination he remained unshaken. He admitted that he had several convictions for selling untaxed whisky in Tennessee and Kentucky. Asked when, he replied, "I didn't keep a dairy" (meaning a diary). Pierce caught the slip and sought to ridicule the witness by asking him about those supposed milk-drinking habits. Fehringer alertly replied, "I used to [drink milk] when I was small, I'm told, but haven't since." [47]

"Where's your home?" Pierce inquired.

Fehringer answered, holding up his old black hat, "Under that."

"Have you no home then?"

"I have not had any for years."

"You have no home nor money?"

"Yes, I have some money, clothes, and other things."

"Where did you get the money, selling whisky?"

"Some of it."

"Where did you get the rest, shooting craps?"

"I got it like you got the ten dollars I [once] gave you to defend me [in another case] and then [you] didn't do it." [48]

Fehringer said he had voluntarily confessed and later had been promised a pardon. The State had also informed him that if he cared to live in the Reelfoot region he would be furnished a military guard, and if not, the State would assist him in settling in another part of Tennessee.[49] Pierce vigorously attempted to discredit Fehringer and impeach his testimony, but the witness remained as facile with his verbal barbs as did the defense attorney. The State could not have expected more of its star witness. Reported New York's *The Sun:* "Night riding can't be conducted in the future when oathbound

45 *News-Scimitar,* December 21, 1908, p. 1.
46 *Nashville Banner,* December 21, 1908, p. 7.
47 *Chattanooga Daily Times,* December 22, 1908, p. 2.
48 *Nashville Banner,* December 22, 1908, p. 3.
49 *Ibid.; The World,* December 23, 1908, p. 4.

riders turn state's evidence to save their own necks. Uncorroborated, the tale of the informer [Fehringer] goes for nothing, and his past is unsavory, but he has struck a blow at the institution of night riding that will be felt wherever it has any vogue in the South. . . ." [50]

The *Nashville Banner* related that while Fehringer was on the stand, a "wild-looking brute" forced his way into the crowd at the back of the courtroom, pulled his revolver, and swore he would "get" the witness before he could tell more. The crisis passed, continued the *Banner,* when calmer minds around the excited intruder persuaded him to abandon his intended assassination.[51] No seizure or arrest? No riot in the courtroom? It hardly seems possible. Reporters covering the trial often stretched the dramatic into the melodramatic in their efforts to outdo their fellow newsmen. They "saw" and reported exciting "sidebars" to their main stories, incidents which under the circumstances could have occurred but did not.

Most of those who attended the trial did predict that some bizarre incident would occur in the courtroom before the hearing terminated. This apprehension led the majority to carry pistols: soldiers, deputies, spectators, and attorneys alike. Periodically a weapon would slip from beneath the belt, where the owner generally carried it, and would thud on the wooden floor causing a nervous laughter to ripple among the spectators. Such accidents likewise occurred at the counsel table. Once an embarrassed Hillsman Taylor, assistant prosecuting attorney, inadvertently dropped his pistol, an incident which caused even the usually staid Judge Jones to chuckle.[52] Contributing to the general apprehension that Night Rider sympathizers might try either to liberate their colleagues on trial or silence a witness was the difficulty in distinguishing between the plainclothed deputies and casually dressed spectators who filled the chamber. A militiaman, Ben James, remembers being on duty as a courtroom guard when a "huge, tough-looking fellow" deliberately drew his pistol while scanning the courtroom scene. Was he a Rider seeking a victim or a deputy suspecting trouble? "Fortunately, he turned out to be a deputy, but one never knew." [53]

50 *The Sun,* December 23, 1908, p. 6.
51 *Nashville Banner,* December 22, 1908, p. 1.
52 Taylor interview.
53 James interview.

Boys in their preteens relieved tensions none by playing soldiers-and-Night-Riders inside the courthouse until an annoyed Judge Jones had them expelled from the building.[54] Furthermore, when the judge realized that the defendants were sitting in court unshackled and guarded by only two deputies, he ordered the prisoners handcuffed and their guard increased to ten.[55]

Throughout the trial, barracks relations between prisoners and soldiers remained amiable. Occasionally, soldiers gave prisoners a forced bath. Two militiamen regularly escorted prisoners to the outhouse, and only once did a prisoner attempt to escape. When the guard placed a round in his rifle and slammed home the bolt, however, the sound alone was sufficient to halt the would-be fugitive.[56] Another prisoner stole a pistol from a sleeping sentry, but before he could use it to advantage, the guard awoke and gave the alarm. Fearful of being caught in possession of the weapon, the prisoner slid it under a soldier's bed from where it was recovered.[57]

A barracks riot was threatened when a black cook wrongly denied a prisoner "seconds" on food. The prisoner leaped over the food counter and was attacking the cook when soldiers arrived to quell the disorder. Captain Ben Capell himself reprimanded the cook: "These men are humans not yet convicted of any crime. If you ever refuse them food again, they won't have to kill you. I will." [58]

The soldiers continued to be their own worst enemies, especially in the careless handling of their rifles. Attempting to protect themselves better, they established a kangaroo court, where those found guilty of mishandling their weapons, or of drunkenness, were either given several smacks across their buttocks with a razor strap or were restricted to barracks. When one soldier ran off a cook at bayonet point because he had been served fatty meat, the "court" awarded the militiaman five swats. Another was restricted for falling asleep on guard duty, and a third punished for missing drill call. The "court," which existed in violation of military regulation, was dis-

[54] *Nashville American,* December 25, 1908, p. 2.
[55] *Chattanooga Daily Times,* December 22, 1908, p. 2.
[56] James interview.
[57] Caksackkar interview.
[58] Capell interview.

banded when an older veteran appealed his "conviction" for drunkenness to Captain Capell.[59]

As the trial continued, prosecution witnesses described in detail the veil of terror that the Night Riders had drawn over the Reelfoot region. Will Russell, another self-admitted Rider, arrived to testify with a pistol protruding from his belt. Caldwell excused his frightened witness in order for him to dispose of his weapon. Then, speaking only in whispers so that Caldwell often had to repeat his questions, Russell explained his activities as a Night Rider and how his life had been threatened since the trial had begun. As the threat could not be attributed to any defendant on trial, Judge Jones struck the remark.[60] A similar ruling occurred during the testimony of D. MacWray, a neighbor of Tid Burton, the Rider indicted when grand jury evidence contradicted his earlier confession. When MacWray declined to comment about his association with Burton, Caldwell inquired if his life had been threatened since his appearance before the grand jury. Defense objected, and the objection was sustained because no such threat could be tied to a defendant.[61]

For the defense, Rice Pierce also investigated threats to witnesses, and under cross-examination Will Russell admitted being "advised" at Camp Nemo to turn state's evidence or else face strong proof held by the State concerning his Night Rider activities.[62]

Mrs. Anna Jackson identified several of the defendants as Night Riders who had whipped her and her family and then had burned her father's home.[63] Mrs. Jackson's testimony was somewhat discredited when she was asked under cross-examination to identify Tid Burton, whom she said she knew. After some hesitation, she pointed to Bud Morris, saying he was Burton.[64] When she finished her testimony, Mrs. Jackson turned to the judge saying, "I will not leave this courtroom without armed protection. I know these

[59] James interview; *Nashville American,* December 15, 1908, p. 2.

[60] *Atlanta Constitution,* December 24, 1908, p. 1; *Chattanooga Daily Times,* December 24, 1908, p. 1.

[61] *Louisville Herald,* December 20, 1908, p. 9 (Section III).

[62] *Chattanooga Daily Times,* December 24, 1908, p. 1; *Atlanta Constitution,* December 24, 1908, p. 1.

[63] *Chattanooga Daily Times,* December 23, 1908, p. 1.

[64] *Nashville Banner,* December 23, 1908, p. 1.

men." [65] Judge Jones then ordered deputies to escort the witness to her residence in Tiptonville.[66]

Mrs. Emma Thurman Johnson described how the Riders had whipped her because she wanted to divorce her Night Rider husband, Joe Johnson. She linked Fred Pinion to the conspiracy,[67] and her testimony led the *Nashville Banner* to editorialize: "Some people have been disposed to invest the Reelfoot Lake Night Riders with the glamour of romance. They were supposed by their sympathizers to have the spirit of knighthood which contended against oppression . . . The evidence [of Mrs. Johnson] destroys the possibility of even this romantic concept." [68]

As the prosecution fully developed its case in court, other prisoners offered to turn state's evidence in exchange for pardons. Caldwell declined, believing that the evidence already presented—including the direct testimony of five former Riders—was strong enough to insure convictions.[69] By Christmas Day the State had virtually completed its presentation, and several newspapers, presuming the Riders' guilt, editorialized for rapid convictions and executions. "If there are not some hangings as the result of the Reelfoot Night Rider trials," said the *Atlanta Journal*, "justice will have gone sadly astray in Tennessee—and the whole South will be the sufferer. It is a situation wherein clemency in the least degree would be rank injustice . . . and a few hangings will exercise a beneficial effect everywhere." [70] Others, while not excusing murder, publicly wondered if the defendants were entirely responsible for the conditions at Reelfoot Lake. *The World* in New York wrote, "These conditions in Tennessee . . . illustrate vividly the danger to society of the law-twisting and law-evading oppression of the unscrupulous strong and the lawless reprisal of the revengeful weak. Responsibility of dealing with both phases of wrong . . . lies with the government." [71]

Christmas brought a recess in the trial and two wagonloads of gifts

[65] *Chattanooga Daily Times*, December 23, 1908, p. 1.
[66] Capell interview.
[67] *Chattanooga Daily Times*, December 22, 1908, p. 1.
[68] *Nashville Banner*, December 22, 1908, p. 8.
[69] *Chattanooga Daily Times*, December 27, 1908, p. 1.
[70] *Atlanta Journal*, December 23, 1908, p. 6.
[71] *The World*, December 24, 1908, p. 8.

to the soldiers. Fireworks exploded over Union City and another elaborate holiday meal was served to both soldiers and prisoners. Visitors were plentiful, including the families of prisoners, who arrived with packed picnic baskets.[72] Many of the lake people remained in the city until December 28 to hear Rice Pierce open his case for the defense which consisted of two basic maneuvers: a long series of alibis that placed the eight men far from the murder scene the night that Rankin died, followed by a parade of character witnesses, who both endorsed the veracity of the defendants and impugned that of the State's witnesses. "As evidence was introduced, it became evident that half the Reelfoot Lake population spent the night of the murder . . . with the other half. . . ." [73] The State agreed that a good deal of visiting went on the night of the murder, specifically that the men, knowing they were going to surprise Rankin and Taylor, left their wives at the homes of friends so that they would be occupied on this well-planned night.[74]

While under direct examination, the defendant Bud Morris spoke loudly and distinctly, but when cross-examined, he mumbled his replies and was repeatedly warned by Judge Jones to speak up.[75] Both Morris and Sam Applewhite denied any affiliation with the Night Riders and gave circumstantial accounts of their whereabouts at the time of the murder.[76] Garrett Johnson admitted that some men of the lake vicinity had gathered on the night of the murder—but at Marsh's store in order to organize an armed posse to repel an anticipated raid from Lake County. Sheriff Easterwood had authorized them to assemble for their protection, Johnson continued, but no masks were worn, and, "I wouldn't know a Night Rider if I saw one." [77]

Each of the defendants remembered distinctly many people who were in their homes the night of the Rankin murder and recalled many incidents that occurred then. Pressed to name people who were present on other nights or recite incidents which happened a few days prior to the murder, they were unable to do so. There was an unusual amount of

[72] *Nashville Tennessean*, December 26, 1908, p. 1.
[73] *The Commercial Appeal*, January 1, 1908, p. 3.
[74] *Chattanooga Daily Times*, December 31, 1908, p. 1.
[75] *Atlanta Constitution*, December 29, 1908, p. 2.
[76] *Chattanooga Daily Times*, December 29, 1908, p. 1.
[77] *Atlanta Constitution*, December 30, 1908, p. 3.

sickness that night too, at least three calls being made for medicine at
homes in which defendants were peacefully sleeping at the time when
self-confessed Riders swore they were murdering Captain Rankin.[78]

Almost every witness introduced by the defense was kin to a defendant, but Pierce explained that families of the lake district had
intermarried for years.[79] Because Judge Jones would not permit
wives to testify for their husbands, Mrs. Bob Huffman substantiated
an alibi for Sam Applewhite, and Mrs. Applewhite returned the
favor for Bob Huffman.[80] Tid Burton and Fred Pinion were the only
defendants not to take the stand. They had made earlier declarations
to the prosecution, and Pierce did not care to have them repeated
under cross-examination.[81]

Defense witnesses swore to a good deal of contradictory evidence.
Joe Hogg, father of self-admitted Rider Herschell Hogg, testified
that his son was in bed at the time Rankin was killed, but previously
young Hogg had admitted holding horses for the Riders at the scene
of the hanging.[82] Sam Baker corroborated the testimony of the elder
Hogg, saying the boy was in bed at his home. Baker had only a vague
memory of visitors who might have come to his house on other
nights; he also could not remember if he had spoken with defense
attorneys the night before he was to testify.[83]

Several defendants depended on the alibi that they had loaded a
wagon of cotton at three o'clock the morning Rankin died and had
taken it to Troy. In rebuttal, the State introduced a receipt book
from the gin to which the cotton was delivered, showing the men had
arrived the morning of the twenty-first of October (the day after the
murder), not the twentieth, as they claimed.[84]

Mrs. Graney, mother-in-law of Wad Morris, another confessed
Rider, swore that Morris went to bed at 10 o'clock the night of the
killing in the same room in which she slept; however, she could not
remember what time he had gone to bed any other night she had

[78] *Courier-Journal*, December 30, 1908, p. 2.

[79] *Ibid.*, December 31, 1908, p. 3.

[80] *Chattanooga Daily Times*, December 31, 1908, p. 1.

[81] *Ibid.*; *Nashville Tennessean*, January 1, 1909, p. 2.

[82] *The Commercial Appeal*, December 30, 1908, p. 14.

[83] *Atlanta Constitution*, December 30, 1908, p. 3.

[84] *Atlanta Journal*, January 4, 1909, p. 2.

known him.[85] Mrs. Wad Morris, introduced to impeach further the testimony of her husband, substantiated the remarks of Mrs. Graney. As Mrs. Morris "left the stand pale and trembling, [she] went into the corridor and sent for the attorney general. 'I have done a great wrong. I have told a lie, my husband was not at home that night. He was with the Riders. I was forced by my relatives to testify as I did. I want to see my husband.' " [86]

Caldwell declined to return Mrs. Morris immediately to the witness chair. He advised her to discuss with relatives the implications of withdrawing her original testimony before she finally decided whether or not to retake the stand. The lady remained firm in her convictions, and the following day when she testified that her brother-in-law had attempted to force her to leave Union City so that she could not be a witness for the State, Caldwell angrily ordered the brother-in-law from the courtroom. Rice Pierce's interjection, "She lied!" drew a rebuke from the attorney general: "I want to go on record as saying that a lady or a child cannot lie. It is abhorrent to nature to say such a thing. They [women] may only be mistaken or misled." [87] Barbed personal insults among the lawyers became so prevalent that on January 1, Jones interrupted the proceedings to say, "This is the first day of the New Year. The glad season of the year, when angels sing of peace and good will, and a clean page is commenced in life's ledgers. I make these remarks as a hint, which the wise will do well to accept." [88]

The petty bickering among counsel, as well as the monotony of the defense testimony, also irked the jurors, who were tiring of their seclusion from public and family affairs. The jurors informed the judge that they objected to further adjournments and advocated longer daily sessions to expedite the trial. Judge Jones sympathized with their feelings but said he already was doing everything possible to accelerate the trial.[89]

The defense particularly aimed to discredit the testimony of the self-confessed Riders. To do this it introduced character witnesses,

[85] *Chattanooga Daily Times*, December 30, 1908, p. 3.
[86] *News-Scimitar*, January 2, 1909, p. 1.
[87] *Ibid.; Atlanta Journal*, January 2, 1909, p. 3.
[88] *News-Scimitar*, January 1, 1909, p. 1.
[89] *Atlanta Constitution*, January 2, 1909, p. 3.

such as Reverend John R. Williams, pastor of the Christian Church of Union City, and Justice of the Peace Stephen Fields. Both Williams and Fields declared that Garrett Johnson had a good reputation, whereas Fehringer was disreputable. Under cross-examination, however, they admitted that since night riding had begun, Garrett Johnson had been suspected of being its leader, and that although Fehringer was a known bootlegger, he had the reputation of telling the truth when accused of a crime.[90] When Caldwell asked Justice Fields if he not only sympathized with the Riders but also rode with them, he provoked a heated denial. The question also rekindled the feud between Pierce and Caldwell and led to another reprimand from Judge Jones, who warned that if the exchanges did not cease, "the counsel table will be short several lawyers one day, and a few distinguished members of the bar will find themselves the enforced guests of the sheriff." [91]

A lull in public interest in the trial, caused by the repetitious defense testimony, was sharply terminated with news of an attempted assassination of Caldwell. *The Commercial Appeal* (Memphis) reported that two shots were fired at the district attorney by a would-be executioner as Caldwell was walking home after a day in court in the company of a Union City newsman.[92] Caldwell, however, said later, "The shooting was the other way around. We tried to shoot someone who evidently was following us." [93] The mystery person, apparently unharmed by the shots, was never identified.

As the trial moved toward its climax, a juror, J. J. Rosson, contracted a severe case of measles, and his temperature became as important as the hearing itself.[94] Should he become too ill to listen to testimony, the court would be forced to declare a mistrial. Not only would this jeopardize the State's case against the present defendants, but it would upset its strategy for prosecuting the remaining Night Rider cases. The State believed that if it could obtain convictions at the current trial, other defendants indicted on night riding charges would plead guilty and thus the nettlesome jury problem

90 *New Orleans Times-Picayune,* January 1, 1909, p. 3.
91 *Ibid.*
92 *The Commercial Appeal,* January 3, 1909, p. 1.
93 *News-Scimitar,* January 3, 1909, p. 1.
94 *The Commercial Appeal,* January 4, 1909, p. 1.

would be eliminated. These guilty pleas were to be accepted in all but those directly involving Rankin's murder (i.e., violations of the Ku Klux Klan Act). Evidence accumulated since the indictments of the eight men on trial had implicated others in the assault on Rankin, and the prosecution intended to try these cases and seek the death penalty for the defendants. All other cases would be open to negotiation with the defense. Reduced charges against most defendants was a probability. Regardless, the State would not seek maximum punishment in the non-Rankin matters. On the other hand, if the trial in progress ended in acquittals or in mistrial, or in any manner short of convictions which could withstand the test of appeals, the prosecution doubted that future juries could be qualified in Obion County to hear Night Rider cases.[95]

Mrs. Rankin appeared in court for the first time on January 4 and the defendants intently watched her as she sobbed on the shoulder of her sister during the alibi testimony. "Mrs. Rankin raised her head a moment, caught sight of the two leering faces [of the defendants] fixed in fascination upon her blackclad figure, shivered convulsively, and turned her tear-stained features from the men charged with her husband's murder." [96]

The defense completed, the lawyers immediately began their final arguments to the jurors. Rosson had to be carried to the courtroom on a stretcher. Caldwell told the panel he was appearing for the State without fee and despite ill health because he was born in Obion County and felt a stigma had been placed upon his birthplace.[97] Referring freely to his boyhood days, when several of those on trial had been among his companions, he asked the jury if he would be there demanding "the blood of my childhood friends" if he were not sworn to uphold justice. Under the circumstances, he regretted that he could only hang about eight and not fifty for the murder of Quentin Rankin.[98] In closing he turned to the defendants and declared: "You have sworn to kill me, but I defy you and all your clan. You can do no more than take my life, and I would gladly lay it down, if

95 *New Orleans Times-Picayune*, January 5, 1909, p. 1; Miles interview.
96 *New Orleans Times-Picayune*, January 6, 1909, p. 1; *News-Scimitar*, January 5, 1909, p. 1.
97 *New Orleans Times-Picayune*, January 6, 1909, p. 1.
98 *Chattanooga Daily Times*, January 8, 1909, p. 2.

by the sacrifice my county and state could be rid of the terrorism and outrages of the night rider mob law." [99]

In closing his calmly delivered, sincere, though emotional appeal, the district attorney urged the jury to eradicate the stain which the murder of Rankin had left upon their county and all Tennessee.

During the short recess which followed Caldwell's address, many spectators stepped forward to commend him on his presentation. However, most present in the packed courtroom had traveled through the snow and bitter zero-degree weather outside principally to hear the oratory of Rice Pierce, knowing that his presentation would be brilliantly contrived and theatrically executed. They were not disappointed, as Pierce skillfully, perhaps even diabolically, portrayed the State, including the governor, as a relentless and ruthless giant which sought to violate the rights and dignity of humble, God-fearing people in the name of supposed justice. "The governor of the state, after sending an army into Obion County to trample on the rights of the people, to snatch honest men from their homes, and bully and abuse them, then offers a reward of $10,000 for the arrest of Rankin's murderers. . ." [100] Finally, the governor "sends for Frank Fehringer and Herschell Hogg and Wad Morris, and he bribes them to perjure themselves and to send honest men to the gallows.[101] Those witnesses, or one of them at least, swore that if Patterson had not offered him the pardon, he would not have made the confession. Just what else he offered them, I do not know, but I believe I have a right to say that he bribed the witnesses to perjure themselves." [102]

Judge Jones did not think that Pierce had any such right, and he interrupted the defense attorney to remind the jury that the record contained nothing to substantiate a charge of bribery against the governor.[103]

As Rosson's condition worsened, opposing counsel agreed to deliver their final remarks to judge and jury in a small room adjoining the courtroom where Rosson lay in bed. He was too sick to be

99 *The World*, January 8, 1909. p. 1.
100 *New Orleans Times-Picayune*, January 7, 1909, p. 1.
101 *Atlanta Constitution*, January 7, 1909, p. 1.
102 *Ibid.*
103 *Chattanooga Daily Times*, January 7, 1909, p. 1.

moved, and there could be no jury deliberation until he was able to consider the evidence along with his colleagues.[104] As a result, the lawyers confined their final statements to a simple outline of their respective positions, comments that were devoid of the sensationalism and emotion which had characterized the entire trial.

The case went to the jury at two o'clock on the afternoon of January 7, but because of Rosson's condition, the panel did not begin its deliberations until 6 p.m.[105] Rice Pierce, awaiting the verdict amidst his clients, remarked, "Boys, we'll have to go to Jackson with this matter. The State's got to the jury." [106] What Pierce intended by the phrase "got to the jury" is not certain. He may have been referring to the manner of grand jury selection or to the loss of his peremptory challenges which he felt had permitted the State to select a trial jury favorable to the prosecution. There never was a public allegation that the State had tampered with the jury. Perhaps Pierce was "just talking," as he was wont to do with his clients. The tenor of his entire statement, however, is clear. Pierce was predicting the conviction of his clients by the Union City jury and the necessity to appeal the decision to the State Supreme Court, which was scheduled to convene in mid-May in Jackson, the seat of Tennessee's western judicial district.

Caldwell had meanwhile traveled to the home of his sister in nearby Fremont to await the jury's verdict. Relatives there were concerned that his extreme nervousness might aggravate his already delicate heart condition.[107] Caldwell himself feared for his life, but not because of heart trouble. "I don't think I'll ever make it back to the courthouse," he told his niece. "Friends of the Night Riders are waiting for me along the road to town, and. . . ." [108] Caldwell's concern proved to be unfounded.

Many out-of-state newspapers, showing little faith in Tennessee justice, predicted acquittals. "No one expects any of the Night Riders

[104] *News-Scimitar,* January 7, 1909, p. 8.
[105] *Chattanooga Daily Times,* January 8, 1909, p. 1.
[106] Morris interview.
[107] Personal interview on November 4, 1956, with Mrs. L. D. Killion, who was with Caldwell at the time.
[108] *Ibid.*

now on trial to be convicted," wrote the *Charlotte Observer*. "The jurors will find a subterfuge to acquit and the defendants will spend the rest of their lives wreaking vengeance on those who testified against them."[109] The *Portland Oregonian* forecast liberty for the defendants and suggested federal intervention to insure public tranquility at Reelfoot Lake.[110]

During the jury's deliberation, Rosson collapsed, and the county physician had to be called to aid him.[111] But the discussion continued, and at 9:15 p.m., the jury announced it had reached its decision. The militia quietly surrounded the courthouse, and a detail of soldiers with revolver holsters open was deployed around the walls of the courtroom with orders to control demonstrations.[112] Then the jury filed in. Six deputies carried Rosson on his bed.[113] The Court requested the verdict, and the jury foreman responded that the panel had found six men—Sam Applewhite, Garrett Johnson, Arthur Cloar, Fred Pinion, Tid Burton and Roy Ransom—guilty of first-degree murder "with mitigating circumstances." It recommended prison sentences of twenty years each for these prisoners. The remaining two defendants, Bud Morris and Bob Huffman, stood convicted of second-degree murder. In each of their cases the jury also recommended twenty-year terms.[114] As far as Morris and Huffman were concerned, Judge Jones, under the law, had no authority to alter their sentences; however, in the cases of the other six, the phrase "mitigating circumstances" included in the jury's verdict left final sentencing to the judge. Jones did not have to accept the recommendation of twenty years for those prisoners. He could either consign the defendants to the gallows or to prison for any term up to life. Most newspapers commenting on the verdict predicted it would be the former.

The *Atlanta Constitution* editorialized:

[109] *Nashville American,* January 9, 1909, p. 4.
[110] *Ibid.*
[111] *Chattanooga Daily Times,* January 8, 1909, p. 1.
[112] *Ibid.*
[113] *Ibid.*
[114] Tennessee, Circuit Court, "Minute Book J," in Records of the Circuit Court (in Obion County Courthouse, Union City, Tenn.), pp. 173–174.

There will be a general feeling of satisfaction . . . in the verdicts of the guilty which will send six of them to the gallows and the other two to the penitentiary for twenty years . . . It [the jury] has fastened the death penalty on Garrett Johnson, the leader . . . In the light of the evidence and all of the circumstances, it can scarcely be questioned that what now remains between sentence and execution is brief time and mere formality.[115]

The *Louisville Herald* was even more direct:

The punishment of the six first-named defendants was left to the court, and may be death or life imprisonment . . . The court will sentence the first named defendants to death.[116]

[115] *Atlanta Constitution,* January 9, 1909, p. 6.
[116] *Louisville Herald,* January 8, 1909, p. 1.

CHAPTER 7

ESCAPE FROM THE HANGMAN'S NOOSE

THE VERDICT IN the Night Rider case disappointed both the prosecution and the defense. The State had anticipated eight first-degree murder convictions,[1] and the defense, outright acquittals or at least a hung jury. The second-degree murder conviction of Bob Huffman was especially puzzling to the prosecution. According to the testimony of Frank Fehringer, Huffman had fired the shot that killed Rankin as he was being drawn up by the rope.[2] Many people regarded the general qualification of "mitigating circumstances" as vague if not inexplicable.

The nation's press expressed widely varied reactions to the verdict. The *Chattanooga Daily Times* was angered and predicted quick pardons for the guilty: "In days gone-by deeds of this kind [Rankin's murder] would have had short shrift at the hands of a healthy-minded jury. . . . These men will go to the penitentiary for three or

[1] *Chattanooga Daily Times,* January 8, 1909, p. 1.
[2] *St. Louis Globe-Democrat,* January 8, 1909, p. 1.

121

four years and then . . . a forgetful community will sign petitions for pardon and a tender-hearted governor will grant it . . ." [3] New York's *World* found that the jury, in examining the motives for night riding, had reflected a general distaste throughout the region for the West Tennessee Land Company's private control of Reelfoot Lake.[4] The *New Orleans Daily Picayune* was pleased: "To the gratified surprise of all friends of law and order . . . , the trial ended in convictions. It was fully expected that in view of the terrorized condition of the section of Tennessee in which the criminals . . . had operated, no jury would be found brave enough to convict them." [5]

The result buoyed Governor Patterson, who called it, "A splendid vindication of the law that will do much to restore the confidence of the people in constitutional authority." Immodestly, he added, "It has been a hard fight . . . but I believe I have conquered the Night Riders and the verdict will . . . kill the organization all over the state." [6]

Throughout the post mortem on the verdict, the defense remained confident it would be reversed.[7] "We will tear this case to pieces in the Supreme Court," assured Rice Pierce, who was expected to center his appeal on the admission of evidence not germane to murder charges.[8]

It became known that the jurors had unanimously agreed the eight defendants were guilty of murder, but there was considerable conflict as to their degree of guilt. Several jurors apparently advocated the death penalty for all defendants; others favored a verdict of second-degree murder with fixed prison terms. The deadlock could have produced a mistrial, but the jury was aware of the improbability of seating a successor to try the case; therefore, it designed a compromise which assured two defendants of substantial prison terms (it is difficult to determine why Huffman and Morris were designated), while placing the others at the mercy of Judge

[3] *Chattanooga Daily Times,* January 9, 1909, p. 4.

[4] *The World,* January 8, 1909, p. 1.

[5] *New Orleans Times-Picayune,* January 9, 1909, p. 6.

[6] *Chattanooga Daily Times,* January 9, 1909, p. 1.

[7] *Nashville Banner,* January 8, 1909, p. 1; *Chattanooga Daily Times,* January 8, 1909, p. 1.

[8] *Nashville Banner,* January 8, 1909, p. 1.

Jones. Knowing the court's predisposition against the defendants, the jurors must have realized this was tantamount to sentencing the six to death, but they wanted to avoid both the stigma of "executioners" and the criticism that inevitably follows the imposition of capital punishment. So they relinquished their sentencing power to the court.[9]

In sentencing the defendants on January 9, Judge Jones found that the testimony in the case "is bristling with perjury" but that the second-degree murder convictions of Huffman and Morris could not be changed by the court. Concerning the others, ". . . in view of the manner in which the life of Quentin Rankin was taken, I can see no mitigating circumstances in this crime. It was not done in the heat of passion, and has none of the element of mitigating circumstances, and that part of the verdict will be disregarded." [10] He then sentenced Johnson, Applewhite, Ransom, Burton, Pinion, and Cloar to death and set their hanging for February 19, 1909. Huffman and Morris each received twenty-year prison terms.[11]

The Riders to be executed received the decision with the same indifference which had characterized all of the defendants throughout the trial. Only Johnson and Pinion allowed themselves faint, half-hearted smiles,[12] while Pinion's mother left the impression she was "a disinterested spectator on a casual visit to the court." [13]

Across the nation, newspapers lauded the verdict of Judge Jones and heralded the end of night riding. "Tennessee has done well to set its foot so firmly upon the hideous reptile of assassination and cowardly assault," wrote the *Louisville Herald.* "We wish that Kentucky was about to deal with its murderers and incendiaries in like fashion." [14] New York's *World* found "something refreshingly vigorous about the Tennessee brand of justice. There were no complicated motives or subtle psychological problems. There was no discussion of brain storms or exaggerated egos and no hint of dementia

[9] Miles interview and Taylor interview.

[10] *New Orleans Times-Picayune,* January 10, 1909, p. 3.

[11] Tennessee, Circuit Court, "Minute Book J," in Records of the Circuit Court (in Obion County Courthouse, Union City, Tenn.), pp. 174–175.

[12] *Nashville American,* January 10, 1909, p. 1.

[13] *Louisville Herald,* January 8, 1909, p. 1.

[14] *Ibid.,* January 10, 1909, p. 4.

furor. No inquiry into the personal history of defendants to discover early symptoms of nervous disease." [15] But *The World* also damned with faint praise, adding with classical Yankee arrogance toward the South: "A community in which murder trials are thus simple almost to the point of rudeness has reason to consider whether it has advanced in civilization proportionally with the older states. There is an obvious need for missionary work in Tennessee." [16]

The *Nashville Tennessean* defensively explained to *The World* that proof was so strong in the Night Rider cases that "there was little room for the introduction of the usual subterfuge concerning insanity and self-defense." [17]

"The law has been vindicated," commented the *McNairy County Independent,* "and doubtless the extreme penalty will ultimately be meted out to as heartless and wicked a set of men as ever pulled a rope." [18] Destruction of the Rider organization was envisioned by the *Nashville American*, and now "life is safe anywhere in Obion County. There may be threats, but they will not be executed. Eight have been convicted, and others will be." [19]

So impressed was the *Milan Exchange* (Tennessee) that it nominated Judge Jones for governor: "Judge Jones has won for himself a home in the hearts of Tennesseans, not only for his fearless work in the recent trial . . . but in his untiring efforts to give everyone justice. And, bye-the-bye, why shouldn't he be the next governor?" [20] When readers suggested that Jones might be better qualified as a State Supreme Court justice, the *Exchange,* while not doubting the judge's potential as a justice, advised, "We still hold that should Tennessee be led by such a man as this, she would regain her place as a leader of the Southern states." [21]

In its motion for a new trial, made immediately after sentencing, the defense alleged that numerous legal errors had been committed by the court during the trial, specifically that jurors McKinney and

[15] *The World,* January 9, 1909, p. 8.
[16] *Ibid.*
[17] *Nashville Tennessean,* January 12, 1909, p. 6.
[18] *McNairy County Independent,* January 15, 1909, p. 1.
[19] *Nashville American,* January 9, 1909, p. 4.
[20] *Milan Exchange* (Milan, Tenn.), January 9, 1909, p. 4.
[21] *Ibid.,* January 16, 1909, p. 4.

Dahnke had expressed fixed opinions before the trial, that testimony of wives on behalf of their husbands had been excluded, the defense deprived of its proper total of peremptory challenges, the jury panel improperly selected, much irrelevant testimony admitted, instructions to the jury misleading and contradictory, and that juror Rosson had been too ill to render an impartial decision.[22]

No one expected Judge Jones to sustain the motion, which the defense had offered only in the normal process of removing the case to the Tennessee Supreme Court. The *St. Louis Globe-Democrat* forecast: "The defense made a motion for a new trial which will be overruled." [23] Its prediction was accurate. By producing jury members as witnesses, the State proved that juror McKinney, far from having a fixed opinion prejudicial to the defendants, had been the juror who insisted upon inclusion of "mitigating circumstances" in the verdict. Contentions as to Rosson and Dahnke then were withdrawn by the defense, and Judge Jones routinely overruled the motion.[24]

The *Nashville American* saw little hope for the defendants in their appeal:

> Counsel for the defense will rely on technicalities for reversal. They will probably find that the Supreme Court is not much given to that sort of thing. Mere technicalities which do not affect the facts of evidence or justice of the verdict have little weight with the Supreme Court, as many criminals seeking to escape punishment on some minor technicality have discovered to their sorrow.[25]

The Riders, however, retained confidence in Rice Pierce's ability to have their convictions reversed, and in accordance with most observers, doubted that another jury could ever be assembled in Obion County to retry the Rankin murder case.[26] Meanwhile, they were transferred to the Madison County jail in Jackson to await the arrival of the Supreme Court.[27]

District Attorney Caldwell, determined to prosecute other Night Rider cases as long as jurors could be secured, hoped to improve

[22] *Nashville Banner*, January 9, 1909, p. 1.
[23] *St. Louis Globe-Democrat*, January 8, 1909, p. 1.
[24] *Atlanta Journal*, January 9, 1909, p. 1.
[25] *Nashville American*, January 10, 1909, p. 4.
[26] Morris interview and Pinion interview.
[27] *Chattanooga Sunday Times*, January 10, 1909, p. 1.

the chances of convictions by trying the defendants individually.[28] Twenty-four accused Riders were still being held in the military barracks at Union City, and further arrests were anticipated. Counsel for both the prosecution and the defense agreed to allow bail for all but those specifically charged with Rankin's murder.[29]

Bypassing eleven "minor" night riding cases previously docketed, the State sought to prosecute Ed Marshall, the prominent farmer who had been freed on $25,000 bail by his brother, the Baptist minister.[30] Caldwell believed that his case against Marshall was substantially strengthened by the confessions of two additional admitted Riders, Will Johnson and Ethelbert Rodgers.[31]

Although much of the tension which accompanied the first trial had subsided by the time Marshall's case was called, the State remained security conscious. Rodgers, for instance, was permitted to visit his parents near the lake the weekend before the trial was to begin, but as a precaution, he was made to post a $25,000 bond, and when he departed, an armed escort went with him.[32]

Selection of a jury in the Marshall case began January 19, and as had occurred in the previous trial, Judge Jones selected the venire. Qualifying the jury again developed into an arduous task. Most prospective jurors claimed fixed opinions and were excused. The prosecution was further handicapped when Caldwell suffered a slight heart attack and temporarily withdrew from the case. Of the 115 veniremen examined the first day, ten were chosen for duty. The defense complained that five of the ten were Union City residents and therefore naturally inclined against the Riders, a contention which the court disallowed.[33] A completed jury was sworn in the following day. The prosecution did not consider it a "good jury," and doubted its willingness to convict, even if confronted by strong proof; however, harassed by the possibility of failing to qualify any jury if overly scrupulous in the examination of its members, the

[28] *The World,* January 8, 1909, p. 1.

[29] *Nashville Banner,* January 12, 1909, p. 12; *Chattanooga Daily Times,* January 14, 1909, p. 1.

[30] *Chattanooga Daily Times,* January 14, 1909, p. 1.

[31] *Ibid.; Nashville Banner,* January 15, 1909, p. 9.

[32] *Hickman Courier,* January 21, 1909, p. 3.

[33] *Chattanooga Daily Times,* January 20, 1909, p. 1; *Nashville Banner,* January 20, 1909, p. 1.

State accepted what it could obtain, despite shortcomings.[34]

Seid Waddell, Fred Carpenter, and Ed Powell offered testimony similar to that they had given at the first trial. They set the stage for Rankin's murder.[35] Two self-confessed Riders, Ransom Slinkard and Charles Russell, failed to appear when called as witnesses, and it was reported Slinkard had left the territory.[36] Frank Fehringer, however, again proved himself a capable witness for the prosecution. He placed the defendant at the murder scene and said Marshall had attempted to dissuade the others from killing Rankin.[37] His testimony was corroborated by Johnson and Rodgers. The former swore that there was no prearranged plan to kill Rankin or Taylor, and that the Riders had agreed that the lawyers would be whipped and forced to walk the fourteen miles to Hickman, Kentucky. Marshall, he continued, had been so persistent in pleading for the lives of the attorneys that Garrett Johnson had threatened to strike him.[38] According to Rodgers, the defendant had also tried to prevent the slaughter of the Walkers.[39]

In his own defense Marshall testified that the Riders threatened to murder his wife and baby and burn his home if he refused to join the band.[40] Failing to dissuade the Riders from hanging Rankin, he said he departed on horseback before the rifle firing began. "I was sobbing, and if Colonel Taylor knew what I did for him, he would embrace me now." [41] Taylor later testified that if Marshall had tried to save his life, he knew nothing about it.[42]

Ben McMurkury had sworn at the first trial that Marshall was with him far from the murder scene when Rankin was slain, but he now admitted that Marshall had told him what to say and that he had perjured himself.[43] The defendant himself acknowledged being at the hanging but insisted he only held the horses of others and had

---

34 Miles interview.
35 *Chattanooga Daily Times,* January 22, 1909, p. 1.
36 *Ibid.,* January 23, 1909, p. 1.
37 *Ibid.*
38 *Ibid.*
39 *Nashville Banner,* January 25, 1909, p. 1.
40 *Chattanooga Daily Times,* January 26, 1909, p. 5.
41 *Ibid.*
42 *Nashville Banner,* January 26, 1909, p. 1.
43 *Chattanooga Daily Times,* January 26, 1909, p. 5.

not gone to Ward's Hotel to seize the victims. Other witnesses contradicted Marshall's account.[44]

As the trial neared its conclusion, Attorney General Caldwell, though physically weakened, returned to assist the prosecution. His brother had been summoned as a character witness for Marshall, but the judge would not allow him to testify.[45] During the final arguments, the wives of Rankin and Marshall, sitting only a short distance apart, were both in tears.[46] Judge Jones charged the jury that even if Marshall had been forced to ride with the band, he was not free of complicity in the clan's activities. Furthermore, if he belonged to a group organized to assault the lawyers, even though he protested against their murders, he was guilty of first degree murder "and should be so adjudged." [47]

The jury was handed the case at five o'clock on the evening of January 27, and six hours later reported itself widely separated in opinion. Ten more hours of discussion failed to break the deadlock, and Judge Jones declared a mistrial. At that moment, the jury stood ten-to-two for acquittal, and those favoring conviction advocated that the charge be reduced to second-degree murder. Jones, apparently annoyed by the failure to reach a verdict, refused to reconsider further bail for Marshall and remanded him to jail.[48]

With the dilemma of further jury selection now beyond immediate solution, pending trials were postponed until May, at least until the Supreme Court had delivered its opinion concerning the appeal of the earlier convictions. In the interim it was decided to place the prisoners in county jails, in order to permit the reduction of military garrisons in Union City and Fort Rankin to twenty men each.[49] The fewer reminders that Obion citizens had of night riding the better for future litigation, reasoned the prosecution. Meanwhile, state legislators were beginning to study the causes of night riding.

Soon after guilty verdicts had been returned against the eight Night Riders, the *Hickman Courier* had editorialized: ". . . The

44 *Nashville Banner,* January 26, 1909, p. 1.
45 *Ibid.*
46 *Chattanooga Daily Times,* January 27, 1909, p. 2.
47 *Ibid.*
48 *Ibid.; Nashville Banner,* January 28, 1909, p. 1.
49 *Chattanooga Daily Times,* January 29, 1909, p. 3.

crime for which the eight men were convicted has been exploited and inflamed by the press until there is only one side to the story. It would be an equally long story to turn the spotlight on the land company—capital covereth a multitude of sins—from whose greed, undoubtedly the present trouble has arisen." [50] By early 1909 the State had already turned its "spotlight" on the land company and was laying the groundwork necessary to attack its claim to private control of Reelfoot Lake.

The legislature opened a regular biennial session in January, 1909, and by the end of the month a joint bill had been introduced permitting the State to purchase the monopoly's interests and declare the lake public.[51] Appearing before the Senate Judiciary Committee, R. Z. Taylor and Judge Harris, principal officers in the land company, opposed the bill on the grounds that it stipulated no specific remuneration for the company. They also reminded the legislators that troops remained at the lake to control lawlessness. Speedy passage of the bill would therefore give recognition to the very movement the State was trying to suppress and would hinder further prosecution of Night Rider cases.[52] The committee took the arguments under advisement and tabled the bill, a decision supported by the *Nashville Banner*, which wanted to see Reelfoot public, but with "due regard for individual rights," meaning the legal property rights of the land company.[53]

Political pressure did not allow Governor Patterson to sidetrack the issue, and in March he publicly endorsed purchase of the lake,[54] and a joint legislative committee was appointed to determine how it could best be accomplished.[55] Convinced of the State's intentions the land company now agreed to sell, or at least lease, lake privileges, although no specific price was mentioned. The *Chattanooga Daily Times* counseled delay until the joint committee had rendered its

---

[50] *Hickman Courier*, January 14, 1909, p. 5.

[51] *Nashville Banner*, January 29, 1909, pp. 5 and 7.

[52] *Ibid.*, February 13, 1909, p. 9.

[53] *Ibid.*, February 16, 1909, p. 6.

[54] *Chattanooga Daily Times*, March 12, 1909, p. 1.

[55] *Ibid.*, March 11, 1909, p. 11; Tennessee, 56th General Assembly, 1909, House, "House Joint Resolution No. 26—Relative to Reelfoot Lake," Adopted by the House on February 17, 1909 (manuscript in the Tennessee State Archives, Nashville).

report. Specifically, the newspaper wanted to know whether the State had to buy the lake or could simply assert control over it. It implied that the question of public versus private ownership of the lake should be restudied.[56] The Supreme Court had sustained private control in 1902, but Supreme Court decisions were not irreversible.

Committee hearings opened at Union City and at various Reelfoot Lake sites in mid-March. Taylor explained the accumulation of grants covering the lake and its shores on which the land company based its claim of private ownership. Harris testified that his father had paid $100,000 for land under the lake and another $20,000 for property around it. Although no stock had as yet been issued, the corporation was said to be capitalized at $125,000. When shares were sold, Harris, who controlled fifty-one per cent, would receive $65,000. An additional $10,000 would go to Harris to improve the lake as a sportsman's resort.[57]

The company's lease to J. C. Burdick, granting him fishing rights, also had to be considered in any settlement. A nine-year agreement, it still had seven years to run. In reviewing his royalties arrangement with the land company, Burdick told the legislators that he had always dealt fairly with the fishermen,[58] and Taylor reminded the committee that there had never been any objection to anyone fishing in the lake or hunting along its shores for pleasure.[59]

A long-time resident of the Reelfoot district, W. W. Wilson, who claimed to have owned the lake in the 1860s, estimated holdings of the land company to be worth only $15,000, and Wilson offered to sell to the State the 5,000 acres he still owned in the area for $450. If the State could not afford the price, he would give the tract away for the public good.[60] Although he had once tried to control the lake for himself, Wilson now favored state ownership. He therefore encouraged the legislature to buy the lake by deliberately undervaluing the land company's property.

Under mounting public pressure to divest itself of its hold on Reel-

---

[56] *Chattanooga Daily Times,* March 16, 1909, p. 4.

[57] *Nashville Banner,* March 17, 1909, p. 7.

[58] *Ibid.*

[59] *Chattanooga Daily Times,* March 17, 1909, p. 1.

[60] *Ibid.; Hickman Courier,* March 18, 1909, p. 5.

foot Lake, the West Tennessee Land Company offered the State exclusive and perpetual hunting and fishing privileges on the lake for $75,000.[61] Members of the investigating committee thought the bid unreasonably high but assumed the corporation could be bargained down, if the legislature decided to lease the property. Speculation was that the State would pay no more than $30,000 for public use of the lake, but the majority of legislators rejected the idea of any lease agreement at all. They favored outright purchase of Reelfoot.

In its recommendations the committee did not seriously consider a lease arrangement with the corporation. It suggested that Reelfoot be transferred to public domain either through direct negotiations or by condemnation proceedings. Representative D. B. Puryear, committee chairman, believed the company held legal title to its property—unless it could be shown that the deeds owned by the corporation had originally been improperly issued by the state of Tennessee and were therefore void. This raised the navigability question. Senator O. K. Holladay, another committee member, argued that the legislature possessed authority to declare the lake navigable and therefore public property.[62] Clearly this was an issue to be decided by the State Supreme Court.

As negotiations continued, Burdick offered to surrender his lease for $10,000. The land company had no objections. It increased its asking price to $85,000 and announced it would give $10,000 of the sum to Burdick.[63] There was also a second lease involved. In December, 1908, the Standard Oil Company had leased 7,000 acres in the lake bottom to probe for oil. J. W. Scott, general agent for Standard Oil, said the company had drilled in seventeen other lakes formed by the earthquakes of 1811 and 1812 "and [had] found oil in every one of them." [64] No oil, as yet, had been found in Reelfoot, but Standard Oil still had another year to run on its lease.[65] The

[61] *Nashville Tennessean*, March 20, 1909, p. 2; *Nashville Banner*, April 9, 1909, p. 1.

[62] *Nashville Tennessean*, March 20, 1909, p. 2.

[63] *Chattanooga Daily Times*, April 2, 1909, p. 1; *Nashville Tennessean*, December 7, 1909, p. 6.

[64] *Nashville American*, December 6, 1908, p. 1; *Nashville Tennessean*, December 7, 1908, p. 6.

[65] *Nashville Banner*, April 9, 1909, p. 1.

year, however, lapsed without the discovery of oil, and Standard Oil's lease presented no problem in the continuing negotiations between the State and land company.

In mid-April the investigating committee rendered its report; it set the course the State was to follow. The legislators found the corporation's bid excessive. Moreover, public opinion demanded a state-owned lake. The lake, the committee felt, was navigable and always had been; therefore it was public property, the grants held by the company were void, and a court would so hold.[66] Several bills drawn by the committee were then adopted by the legislature. The first empowered the attorney general to settle conflicting claims to property under and around the lake. This involved the annulment of suits brought against the land company by individuals who maintained that they owned parcels of land at the lake.[67] The second authorized the attorney general to proceed with condemnation suits against anyone holding valid titles to land within the Reelfoot Lake area all of which was to be designated as a public game and fish preserve.[68] A third law regulated fishing and hunting at the lake by fixing costs for the privilege of working the lake for profit but stipulating that hunting and fishing for pleasure were to be free.[69]

Despite the strongly adverse committee report and the subsequent legislation, the land company, which had a strong lobby within the legislature, continued to press for a lease agreement with the State. In May, Representative Frank Langford of Davidson County (Nashville) introduced a bill that authorized the State to pay $60,000 (a $75,000 figure has been scratched out on the original document) for a perpetual lease to rights on the lake, an amount which represented only a $15,000 reduction from the company's first proposal and did not include settlement of Burdick's claim. After passing two readings (a third was needed for adoption), the measure was rejected on May 26.[70] Neither side ever again raised the possibility of

[66] *Ibid.*, April 16, 1909, p. 11.
[67] Tennessee, *Public Acts* (1909), Ch. 371.
[68] *Ibid.*, Ch. 534.
[69] *Ibid.*, Ch. 463.
[70] Tennessee, 56th General Assembly, 1909, House, "H. R. 806: Bill to purchase easement to fish and hunt on Reelfoot Lake . . ." (manuscript in the Tennessee State Archives, Nashville).

a lease for the Reelfoot property. What the legislators wanted before spending any public funds on lake property was a new Supreme Court opinion on the navigability issue.

While the state legislature had been contemplating the purchase of Reelfoot Lake, a relative calm pervaded Obion County. Citizens openly speculated on the outcome of the appeal of the Night Rider cases soon to be considered by Tennessee's Supreme Court. Juror Rosson recovered from his measles, although he was not allowed to leave his specially prepared bedroom in the courthouse for several days following the trial.[71] A second juror, Mansfield Haroldsen, a prominent farmer, was apparently so troubled by the entire Night Rider episode that he went insane and hanged himself.[72]

Five masks and two robes worn by Riders were discovered by militiamen in a tin bucket on Nick's Towhead, an island in Reelfoot Lake. Because the Riders had burned most of their regalia following Rankin's murder, the State had been unable to introduce substantial physical evidence of night riding at the first trial and welcomed the examples for future prosecutions. The owners of the disguises were identified by Frank Fehringer, but their names were not revealed pending their arrests.[73]

Will Watson, indicted in Lake County as the leader of the Riders who had whipped Squire Wynne, was to stand trial in March in Tiptonville on a charge of violating the Ku Klux Klan Act. The sudden illness of his lawyer, Rice Pierce, however, forced postponement of that trial.[74] By the time that Judge Jones opened the May term of court in Obion, Pierce had recovered and announced that the defense was prepared to try any Night Rider cases the prosecution cared to present. This time it was the court which postponed the proceedings, preferring to await the Supreme Court's decision on the appeals before attempting to try other Night Rider cases.[75]

Prisoners held in the military barracks at Union City were transferred to jails in Dyersburg, Dresden, and Union City, although three remained in the barracks a few days longer because they had

[71] *Chattanooga Daily Times*, January 9, 1909, p. 1.
[72] *Ibid.*, May 15, 1909, p. 1.
[73] *Hickman Courier*, January 28, 1909, p. 4.
[74] *Chattanooga Daily Times*, March 8, 1909, p. 1, and March 9, 1909, p. 1.
[75] *Nashville Banner*, May 5, 1909, p. 4.

contracted measles.[76] As they were turned over to their jailers, many prisoners thanked the soldiers for their friendship.[77] Riders who had turned state's evidence also were retained in county jails but received special considerations. Herschell Hogg, for instance, was given "trusty" privileges at Dresden and occasional permission to visit his family at home.[78] By mid-May the remaining troops at Fort Rankin and in Union City were ordered home. Civil authorities, it was deemed, had matters well in hand.[79]

The public calm did not hold for all Tennessee, for night riding had erupted in Humphreys County (Middle Tennessee) in connection with the peanut-growing industry. Many of the tactics employed by Reelfoot's Riders had been adopted by the clansmen in Humphreys, and Governor Patterson had been forced to send thirty national guardsmen to the scene.[80] Eighteen men were arrested in Humphreys County as Night Riders. They could have been tried under the Ku Klux Klan Act, and, if convicted, sentenced to be hanged. Instead, they were convicted of simple misdemeanors, fined $500 each and jailed for ten days.[81] Yet night riding continued in Humphreys County. When Patterson offered a $250 reward for the arrest and conviction of anyone connected with night riding in that county, he inspired reckless bounty hunting. One posse arrested thirty-two men, of whom only eleven were subsequently convicted of night riding. But for his work, the head of the posse collected a fee of $2,750 from the state treasury.[82] Some people blamed the continuance of night riding in Humphreys on the light penalties assigned there by the courts. These citizens claimed that the way to stop night riding was to hang a few of the clansmen. This attitude focused the nation's attention on Jackson where the lives of the six convicted Night Riders were at the mercy of the state's highest court.

The Tennessee Supreme Court heard the appeal of the original

[76] *Hickman Courier*, February 4, 1909, p. 4.

[77] *Ibid.*

[78] *Nashville Banner*, March 13, 1909, p. 9.

[79] *Chattanooga Daily Times*, May 14, 1909, p. 1; *Nashville Banner*, May 17, 1909, p. 1.

[80] *Nashville Banner*, April 12, 1909, p. 1; *Chattanooga Sunday Times*, April 11, 1909, p. 1; and *Chattanooga Daily Times*, April 13, 1909, p. 1.

[81] *Nashville Banner*, May 12, 1909, p. 12.

[82] *Ibid.*, May 15, 1909, p. 4.

Night Rider convictions from May 20 to May 23. The prisoners arrived in court showing the effects of their confinement. Their march from the Jackson jail to the courtroom marked the first time they had been out of their cells since January, and the normally robust outdoorsmen appeared pale and drawn. In its plea for reversal, the defense relied on the series of errors alleged in its motion for a new trial plus the alibis of the defendants. After hearing the carefully outlined arguments of the attorneys for both sides, the court took the case under advisement and promised a decision within two weeks.[83]

The Supreme Court took more than a month to prepare its conclusions, which were announced on July 3. Despite their physical frailties, the heavily guarded defendants appeared confident of their future as they were led into the chamber to learn their fate. Friends and sympathizers of the accused attended by the score, and the prisoners greeted them quietly, shaking their hands.[84] Attorney General Caldwell told his colleagues that the defendant Arthur Cloar would be absent because he was ill, and added nervously, "They are going to reverse this case, and if they do, it's all over. I don't believe we can ever get another jury to try them. This case means more to me than any living man." [85]

It took Special Justice Harry A. Craft of Memphis more than an hour to read the decision. He had been appointed to hear the case after Justice M. M. Neil had recused himself because he was a relative of Mrs. Rankin. The stillness in the courtroom was broken only by the droning voice of Justice Craft: [86]

". . . The court is of the opinion that there is manifest error in the record, to wit: in the organization of the grand jury by which indictments against the plaintiffs in error were returned, and in selection of the petit jury by which the plaintiffs in error were tried . . . ." [87]

The Supreme Court noted that when calling special terms of

[83] *Chattanooga Daily Times,* May 21, 1909, p. 1.
[84] *New Orleans Times-Picayune,* July 4, 1909, p. 13.
[85] *McNairy County Independent,* July 9, 1909, p. 2.
[86] *New Orleans Times-Picayune,* July 4, 1909, p. 13.
[87] Tennessee, Supreme Court, "Docket of the Supreme Court, Minute Book 44" (manuscript in the office of the Supreme Court Clerk, Tennessee State Courthouse, Jackson, Tenn.).

court such as that convened in Union City, the law "plainly imposed the duty upon the judge to appoint three justices to select and designate the persons to be summoned for jury service at such term, and no discretion is vested in the judge as to omitting the performance of this duty." [88] Judge Jones had selected the jurors from bystanders and with them had organized the grand jury. "The justices should have selected a panel of twenty-five, from which thirteen would be chosen for service by chance," continued the opinion. "Even if the judge did choose the venire [of twenty-five], he should have left selection of the actual jurors to chance." [89]

The Supreme Court also found that Judge Jones erred in permitting eleven of the thirteen members of the grand jury to serve because they had been members of an Obion County grand jury within the previous two years and were therefore ineligible.[90]

Concerning selection of the trial jury, the high court found: "There is nothing whatsoever in the record to show any intention on the part of the defendants, or their counsel, to waive so important a right to challenge 192 veniremen instead of twenty-four . . ." [91] Judge Jones had committed "serious error" in denying the defense its full twenty-four challenges for each defendant. As a result, jurymen served "who would never have been accepted by the defendants, had they possessed the right to challenge." [92] Some jurors who had expressed opinions hostile to the defendants were accepted. Also, the defense was forced to spend peremptory challenges on prospective jurors who had fixed opinions formed by reading newspapers and talking with those who claimed to know the facts of the killing. The court believed these should have been dismissed for cause. It was also found that Judge Jones had erroneously curtailed the defense's examination of prospective jurors and had put too much emphasis on statements of prospective jurors who admitted having opinions but said they could still render a just verdict.[93]

Justice Craft concluded, "It is unnecessary to consider or pass upon any other assignments of error." [94] This statement did not

[88] *Nashville Tennessean,* July 7, 1909, p. 10.

[89] *Ibid.*

[90] *Ibid.*

[91] *Ibid.*

[92] *Ibid.*

[93] *Ibid.*

[94] *Nashville Banner,* July 7, 1909, p. 10.

preclude the probability that other errors existed in the trial record, but meant the Supreme Court had found sufficient cause to reverse the convictions in reviewing the initial allegations of the defense. The case was then remanded to Obion County for retrial. The prisoners were returned to Union City, where they could seek bail and have their cases rescheduled for trial.[95]

Courtroom spectators welcomed the decision with raucous applause but were quickly stilled by deputies.[96] Caldwell hung his head in his hands. With thirty-two alleged Night Riders in jail awaiting trial and twenty-one others out on bail, the *McNairy County Independent* justly commented, "The opinion was fraught with more than the saving of six necks." [97]

Despite the prevalence of error uncovered by the Supreme Court, its decision to reverse was far from unanimous. It had been adopted by only a three-to-two vote of the five judges, with Justices Craft, W. D. Beard, and Bennett D. Bell concurring, while John K. Shields and W. K. McAlister dissented.[98] Apparently, no minority report was read in court, nor were details of this position reported in the press. It appears that Justices Shields and McAlister declined to reverse on the basis of technical errors in trial procedure when the preponderance of evidence proved the guilt of the defendants. This issue became the core of the strident controversy which followed the Supreme Court's decision: When strong evidence proves guilt, should a murder conviction be reversed because of technical failures in courtroom practice?

The majority of newspapers commenting on the Supreme Court's opinion thought not. In fact, Tennessee's high court was subjected to harsh criticism, bordering on contempt. *The Commercial Appeal* wrote: "Yesterday was a day of triumph for murder and lawlessness . . . That justice may get what is due it for the murder of Rankin is today almost a barren hope. Rankin was murdered, yet the machinery of the law is between his murderers and the gallows." [99] Granting that the court was technically correct in its contention, the news-

[95] *New Orleans Times-Picayune*, July 4, 1909, p. 13.
[96] *Ibid.*
[97] *McNairy County Independent*, July 9, 1909, p. 2.
[98] *Ibid.*
[99] *The Commercial Appeal*, July 5, 1909, p. 6.

paper then noted the difficulty of obtaining an impartial juror in sensational crimes "unless he was deaf, dumb, and blind." The newspaper concluded: "This opinion of the Supreme Court is a splendid thing for the wretches who killed Rankin like a dog; in its technical hair-splitting exaggeration of the importance of trivial things, foreign to the body of the crime, it is a sickening shock to justice." [100]

Others were scarcely less furious. "By a stroke of a pen the Supreme Court nullified good work done in bringing the murderers to justice," said the *Atlanta Constitution*.[101] ". . . If technicality is to be permitted to override justice, administration of the law will lie in the hands of the strong, and there will be no need of courts. . . ." [102] The *Trenton Herald Democrat* (Tennessee) called the decision "little short of a crime," and predicted it would "set back administration of justice in Tennessee more than fifty years." [103] The *Fayette Falcon* wrote: "Justice in Tennessee [has] . . . received the most severe slap-in-the-face it has had in many a day. . . . All praise to Judges McAlister and Shields who dissented. . . . The people of Tennessee will hardly forget Bell and Beard when the next election comes." [104]

In its anger, the *McNairy County Independent* certainly ventured into contempt, though it was not cited: "The courts of Tennessee, and many other states, are made up of politicians and not men learned in the law. The people have lost all confidence in their decisions and well they might." [105] Because of a lack of "stern justice," the *Independent* foresaw that in future crimes as blatant as the Rankin murder, justice would be meted out "by an outraged public." [106] Indeed, the *New Orleans Daily Picayune* seemed to advocate lynch-mob justice: ". . . When the law has not a strong enough hand to deal with some sorts of crime, it does well to get out of the way and allow society to work out its problems as best it may by primitive methods." [107]

[100] *Ibid.*
[101] *Atlanta Constitution*, July 6, 1909, p. 6.
[102] *Ibid.*
[103] *Trenton Herald-Democrat*, July 8, 1909, p. 1.
[104] *Fayette Falcon*, July 9, 1909, p. 4.
[105] *McNairy County Independent*, July 9, 1909, p. 1.
[106] *Ibid.*
[107] *New Orleans Times-Picayune*, July 4, 1909, p. 8.

The *Nashville American* saw the decision as "evidence of the unwisdom of hurried trials of men accused of crime in times of great popular excitement;" [108] and the *Nashville Tennessean* advocated "a study of our system of practice and procedure in criminal trials with a view to active reforms." [109]

Even Attorney General Caldwell publicly censured the decision:

> I would not complain, if they had gone into the facts . . . and seen proper to say that the facts did not warrant a conviction, but for them to reverse so important a case on mere technicalities occurs to me as being a travesty on justice . . . I may be wrong, but in my opinion these three judges have committed a judicial blunder such as had not occurred in a hundred years of Tennessee jurisprudence. Of course, I accord them honesty and sincerity, but the God of justice pities their judgement.[110]

Caldwell remarked that he saw no possibility of again bringing the defendants to trial because of the jury question. "Retributive justice must be left to an avenging God." [111]

Caldwell's rebuke was too strong for the *Nashville American* which answered the attorney general, "Our faith in the Supreme Tribunal is strengthened by its conviction that maintenance of law and strict adherence to legal procedure was of far more moment than concurrence in a verdict reached contrary to proper legal procedure." [112]

A properly balanced conclusion to the general debate would seem to be that of W. M. Miles, the Union City attorney who was a spectator at the Rider trial: "The entire proceeding was a case of necessity and necessity often knows no law. There were quite a few judicial errors committed, and there is no doubt but that Judge Jones stretched the legal blanket to get convictions. But heroic remedies had to be applied to a drastic situation." [113]

Unfortunately for the State's case, the Supreme Court did not allow these "heroic remedies" to include evasion of the law, no matter how slight the deviation. Judge Jones manipulated legal procedure sufficiently to insure that the case went to trial and was encour-

---

[108] *Nashville American*, July 4, 1909, p. 4.
[109] *Nashville Tennessean*, July 7, 1909, p. 4.
[110] *Atlanta Journal*, July 5, 1909, p. 2.
[111] *Ibid.*
[112] *Nashville American*, July 6, 1909, p. 4.
[113] Miles interview.

aged to do so by the prosecution. Had all legalities been technically observed, the trial might never have occurred. From the outset, the State was in a difficult legal position. It could not proceed individually against defendants because of the impossibility of securing successive juries once the core of its evidence had become public. On the other hand, by trying the accused jointly, it faced the problem of selecting a "good" jury despite an overpowering number of peremptory challenges allowed by the defense. This predicament spawned the strategy which led to the limitation of the defense's challenges. Certainly the State recognized the legal dangers inherent in a move which deprived the defense of fundamental rights in a murder trial. In sustaining the State's gamble, Judge Jones invited the reversal which occurred. When the gamble failed, so did the prosecution's case against Reelfoot's Night Riders. Rankin's tragic murder was to go unavenged.

CHAPTER 8

REELFOOT LAKE IS FREE

THE DAY (JULY 3) that the State Supreme Court delivered its opinion in the Night Rider cases was another tense one in Union City. Hundreds of friends and relatives of the defendants had trekked to the city from the lake region to learn of the decision by telegraph. "Good people" of Union City stayed off the streets, and town authorities feared that if the court upheld the convictions— thereby condemning the six men to death—there would be ugly demonstrations, difficult to control. News of the reversal, however, was met with joyous rebel yells, hardy backslaps, and firm handshakes among the lake folk. Women cried, and curiously, a good many citizens of Union City congratulated the Reelfoot residents on "their victory." Perhaps this was because they felt, as did many, that the defendants had received a far from fair trial in Judge Jones' court. Most of the lake people remained in Union City that night to celebrate; a few hurried back to Samburg and other settlements around the lake to spread the "good news." [1]

[1] *New Orleans Times-Picayune,* July 4, 1909, p. 13; Miles interview.

A disconsolate Attorney General Caldwell meanwhile considered dismissal of all the remaining night riding cases because of the improbability of obtaining a jury to try them.[2] Observers generally agreed with him, and when the State asked Judge Jones to postpone forty cases set for the July term, he concurred, although he continued to deny bail for the prisoners.[3]

Despite the apparent futility of bringing other night riding cases to trial, the State did make a conscientious attempt. On November 15, 1909, the Obion County Grand Jury returned new indictments charging murder against Arthur Cloar and Garrett Johnson, two of the eight involved in the reversal.[4] When the cases came to trial at the end of December, the jury became hopelessly deadlocked in its deliberation, and Judge Jones declared another mistrial. The court reset these murder trials for January, 1910; however, there is no further mention of the proceedings against Cloar or Johnson on either the Obion County court docket or in the court's minute book. Ninety new indictments returned against Riders were scheduled for trial in February, 1910,[5] but were continued to May and then to September of that year,[6] when they also were dismissed.[7] In the fall of 1910, Judge Jones recognized the State's predicament and began to doubt the practicality of bringing any of the remaining Night Rider cases to trial. For the first time in the entire proceedings against the Riders he granted bail to all defendants. The prosecution finally collapsed in 1910, and the court dismissed all indictments against alleged Night Riders and discharged the defendants from bail.[8]

Release of the suspects aroused fear for the witnesses who had testified against the Riders. Governor Patterson and his aides had anticipated that murder convictions in the Rankin case would elim-

[2] *Nashville Banner,* July 5, 1909, p. 10.

[3] *Ibid.,* July 6, 1909, p. 2; *McNairy County Independent,* July 16, 1909, p. 2.

[4] Tennessee, Circuit Court, "Minute Book J," in Records of the Circuit Court (in Obion County Courthouse, Union City, Tenn.), p. 476.

[5] *Ibid.*

[6] Tennessee, Circuit Court, "Minute Book K," in Records of the Circuit Court (in Obion County Courthouse, Union City, Tenn.), pp. 60–61.

[7] Taylor interview.

[8] *Ibid.*

inate any thoughts of reprisals against witnesses. But with the former defendants at liberty, the possibility of revenge created new concern. Judge Jones received a letter from St. Louis warning that he would be assassinated if it took ten years to do the deed. The same note insisted that the entire trial jury would be killed, the Union City courthouse blown up, and the city reduced to ashes. Judge Jones, who walked Union City unarmed and unprotected during the entire litigation, considered this latest threat a bluff and ignored it.[9] The *New Orleans Daily Picayune,* however, advised witnesses and jurors to protect their lives by leaving the Reelfoot district. "If no one is left in the country upon whom the alleged outlaws can be revenged, they will return to Reelfoot, take possession, and if not interfered with, make no further trouble." [10] The *New York Tribune* was less pessimistic, writing that it was "hardly possible that any bodily harm" would come to witnesses, "because by their conduct they have greatly diminished the power of the organization." [11]

As far as is known, no reprisals ever were taken by former Riders against witnesses who had testified against them—including those clansmen who had turned state's evidence.[12] Their resentment (even to the present day) appears to have been directed only against Frank Fehringer, who they felt confessed the secrets of the Night Riders in order to collect the $10,000 reward offered by the State (although neither he nor any one else ever collected it).[13] Had the former Riders later apprehended Fehringer in their territory, they might have fulfilled their vow to murder him, but the bootlegger reportedly moved to St. Louis, Missouri, and never reappeared at Reelfoot Lake.[14]

Other Night Riders who were state's witnesses returned to their homes without apparent stigma. None is known to have accepted the governor's offer of safe escort and relocation in another part of Tennessee. Two factors seem responsible for the reasonable behavior of the Riders following the trials. First, they had neither antici-

---

[9] *McNairy County Independent,* July 9, 1909, p. 2.
[10] *New Orleans Times-Picayune,* July 4, 1909, p. 8.
[11] *New York Tribune,* December 28, 1909, p. 6.
[12] Morris interview and Pinion interview.
[13] *Chattanooga Daily Times,* March 23, 1909, p. 1.
[14] Morris interview and Pinion interview.

pated the raw power of the militia nor the vigorous sincerity of the State in prosecuting them. In short, "They had experienced a close call with the gallows, and had no stomach for further night riding." [15] Second, the State was progressing in its determination to make Reelfoot a public preserve.

For more than two years, beginning in the spring of 1909, the State and the West Tennessee Land Company attempted to negotiate their differences concerning ownership of the lake; however, the endeavor had proved futile. The monopoly reaffirmed its determination to retain its property, although the $65,000 offer for perpetual hunting and fishing rights stood. But the legislature refused to pay this amount, especially for only long-term privileges. The State wanted to own Reelfoot, but it shied from condemnation proceedings, apprehensive that a condemnation court would commit taxpayers to a purchase price the State could ill afford to pay. The alternative was to seek ownership of the lake through a favorable court decision on the navigability question.

The ensuing court fight became as much political as legal, and the land company as well as the State were represented by both superior legal talent and politically influential lobbyists.[16] Public sympathy was somewhat ambivalent. Citizens desired a state-controlled Reelfoot Lake, but they believed the land company should be fairly compensated for its loss. Considerable debate concerned the matter of "fair compensation." [17]

The State proceeded against the land company in the Chancery Court of Obion County, asking the court to void the corporation's titles on grounds they had been illegally issued for property which constitutionally belonged in the public domain. The West Tennessee Land Company relied on the navigability decision of 1902 for its defense. Chancellor C. P. McKinney upheld the land company, ruling that it held valid title to lake property. This decision was affirmed by the Tennessee Court of Appeals, and the State's petition for a rehearing reached the Supreme Court sitting in Jackson in April, 1913.[18]

15 Capell interview.
16 Taylor interview.
17 *Ibid.*
18 McGill and Craig, *JTAS,* VIII, p. 19.

At the outset, the high court decided to consider only the navigability issue.[19] It did not intend to investigate the titles of the land company or in other ways embroil itself in the negotiations between the State and corporation. Like so many of the legal technicalities encountered during the Night Rider episode, that concerning navigability of the lake was a fine one, capable of varying interpretations. Tom Southworth, the Union City photographer whose personal acquaintance with the principals conducting the Rider trial had accorded him the exclusive privilege to take pictures, again found himself in a unique position. As the only professional photographer familiar with the lake area, Southworth was employed by each side to "prove" its case pictorially. For the State, he took pictures of open stretches of water as evidence of the lake's navigability. On the other hand, the land company hired him to photograph areas clogged with tree stumps and weeds which impeded navigation.[20]

In a split decision, with Chief Justice M. M. Neil dissenting, the Supreme Court sustained the State and ruled Reelfoot Lake to be navigable—as it always had been. It followed that the state of Tennessee had improperly issued private deeds to public domain below the lake's surface; therefore, such deeds were void. The justice found that Reelfoot was sufficiently large and deep to handle most of the ships plying the Cumberland and Obion Rivers, and that the presence of stumps and trees in the water, although hindering navigation, did not affect the lake's capacity or render it unnavigable in a legal sense. Basically, the court continued, the Reelfoot Lake question concerned ownership rather than commerce and travel, and the public had rights, such as fishing and ownership, in streams which were technically navigable.[21] "Authorities supporting the decision in *Webster versus Harris* [the 1902 case] do not represent the great weight of American authority, and some of them are not applicable." Furthermore, "as the lake has capacity for navigation in the technical sense, the rights of the public attach to it, to its use, and to its fisheries, so that it is incapable of private ownership, and the

[19] *State, ex. rel. Charles T. Cates, Jr.,* v. *West Tennessee Land Company et al.,* 19 Cates (Tenn.), 580 (1913).

[20] Southworth interview.

[21] *State* v. *West Tennessee Land Company,* 19 Cates (Tenn.), 588–596, *passim* (1913).

state owns it in trust for all the people, and cannot alienate it away." [22]

The court's ruling excluded grants issued by the state of North Carolina before Reelfoot Lake existed. "The mere fact that they [specifically the four former Doherty tracts held by the land company] have become submerged by a body of navigable water does not deprive the owners of their title to the land . . . . This does not include the right of detaining fish, or preventing their free movement [over the Doherty property], and only includes the exclusive rights to take fish in waters over these grants as they may be found by their natural inclination." [23]

Noting that a small steamer once had experienced difficulty navigating the lake and had sunk, Chief Justice Neil dissented from the majority opinion, finding the lake too shallow and cluttered to be declared navigable. Excepting two or three places where it was four feet deep, Justice Neil noted the water was only inches deep around the shoreline, and that navigable water generally lay at least 100 feet from shore. He suggested the State buy or condemn and pay for the lake "just like any other property it needs." [24]

With the bulk of the Reelfoot land in its possession via the Supreme Court's ruling, the State then instituted condemnation suits to obtain the remainder—the Doherty tracts. This matter was settled out of court. The West Tennessee Land Company received $25,000 for the four adjoining grants, an amount approximating that which the State had offered for all of the monopoly's holdings before the navigability issue had gone to court. Of the total, $15,000 was paid for the Obion portion and $10,000 for the section in Lake County. [25] Condemnation authorities had first appraised the Obion area at $22,500, but the State appealed this ruling, and the land company agreed to the lower figure. [26]

Throughout the litigation, J. C. Burdick's Reelfoot Fish and Game Company had retained its lease to the fishing concession on the lake, and in 1913 it still had three years to run. Before the Supreme

---

[22] *Ibid.*
[23] *Ibid.*, 598.
[24] *Ibid.*, pp. 644–61.
[25] *News-Scimitar*, January 6, 1914, p. 1.
[26] *Nashville Tennessean*, September 16, 1923, p. 2.

Court's navigability decision, lower courts had sustained Burdick's right to control the wholesale fish business at the lake. Even after the Supreme Court's ruling, Burdick legally controlled fishing over the Doherty tracts. This situation forced the State to negotiate for the purchase of Burdick's lease. The matter was settled out of court in 1914. Burdick received $2,000,[27] and the State could now claim full and legal control of Reelfoot Lake. Total cost for the property and for attorney's fees incurred in the legal maneuvering to obtain it amounted to $36,000.[28]

Unforeseen at the time of the purchase was the problem created by the fluctuating level of the lake, a condition which left the strip of land between low and high water marks in dispute. A levee built at the south end of the lake in 1917 failed to maintain the water at a constant level, and in flood seasons the dam backed up water onto the property of riparian owners, ruining acres of cultivated farmland. In solving this dilemma, the state legislature in 1925 authorized purchase of a wide band of property around the lake which was designated as part of the Reelfoot Lake Park and Fish and Game Preserve.[29] A permanent, concrete spillway with adjustable floodgates was constructed in 1931 to maintain the lake at a constant level.[30]

Social conditions around the lake had meanwhile become stabilized. A few former Night Riders, although not admitting their part in the gang's activities, bragged about the deeds of the organization and its ultimate success in "freeing" Reelfoot Lake. Judge Harris, an excellent swimmer said to be in good physical condition, drowned in the lake in 1913. The tragedy created rumors that the Riders had taken final revenge against him. Officially Harris' death was described as accidental, and no competent evidence has yet refuted that finding.[31]

For the most part, former Riders and their kin, still fearing prosecution by the State, said nothing of the clan and its purpose.

[27] Cecil C. Humphreys, "The Formation of Reelfoot Lake and Consequent Land and Social Problems," *The West Tennessee Historical Society Papers*, XIV (1960), 61–2.

[28] *Nashville Tennessean*, September 16, 1923, p. 2.

[29] McGill and Craig, *JTAS*, VIII, 20.

[30] *Ibid.*

[31] Taylor interview.

For six decades this reluctance has persisted. Yet most people of the lake district are quietly proud of the boldness displayed by the Riders and still believe the organization was justified in its goals.

The animosity spawned between Lake and Obion Counties during the night riding era left a residue which is evident today. The Obion side of the lake is often referred to as "Night Rider country," and visitors are warned not to cross the natives.

Time, motels, communications, and profits are eroding the attitudes that for so long shielded the district from modernization. Older generations at the lake still manifest their individuality with an air of gruffness toward outsiders and a veneer of mysticism concerning the Night Riders. The trend toward updated living, however, is irreversible. A good deal of genuine hospitality now is evident as younger entrepeneurs welcome both visitors and business to the region that preserves its romantic air and historical presence which are the final legacies of the Night Riders of Reelfoot Lake.

AFTERWORD TO THE 2003 EDITION

I FIRST BECAME ACQUAINTED with Reelfoot Lake in the mid-1950s, while working as a reporter for the now defunct but then quite lively and popular *Memphis Press-Scimitar*. I covered the dramatic civil rights story of the Reverend Martin Luther King's visits to the city, as well as the spectacular emergence of a hip-gyrating youngster named Elvis Presley. Part of my beat included Memphis State University, which was considering plans for racial integration, and history department professors proved to be my most reliable informants. One day the history chair, Enoch L. Mitchell, a scholar and gentleman if ever there was one, suggested that I pursue a master's degree in history. "Why?" I inquired. "Because you can write a good story as a thesis." "What story?" I asked. "The night riders of Reelfoot Lake," came the response. And I was hooked.

All I knew about Reelfoot at the time was the mystery surrounding it. I had heard the admonition to stay away. People living on the lake were said to be brooding and malicious; supposedly, they did not like outsiders asking questions. Some of those involved in the night riding still lived around the lake and feared they might yet be liable for criminal prosecution. The descendants of participants stood ready to defend the honor and reputations of their kinfolk. Under such circumstances, an investigator, scholarly or otherwise, needs a friendly and reliable local contact to make introductions. Dan McKinnis, then the country judge for the Reelfoot region, proved to be my guardian angel, even if on occasion we had to spend some time hunkered down behind a fallen tree until the proper introductions could be made. In the end, enough people around Reelfoot were sufficiently amiable, and I was able to weave together the story. Frankly, they saw nothing shameful in the night riding that had convulsed the region, led to the calling out of the state militia, shaken state politics, and made headlines across the nation. In fact, they looked upon it with considerable satisfaction, even pride.

Writing *Night Riders of Reelfoot Lake* changed my life. It introduced me to the struggle between those fulfilled by a traditional way of life handed down from their forebears and those who seek radical change in the name of betterment and modernity. It led me to believe that there is mystery in the world that cannot be fathomed. Not everything can be understood, and I am willing to let it go at that. Finally, it left me with an abiding interest in history that led me to pursue a Ph.D. in history at the University of Texas and then into academia at San Diego State University—teaching, researching, writing, debating with colleagues—until retirement a few years back. Throughout my career, my writing has been centered on the lessons I learned at Reelfoot Lake: the impact of a modernizing world on ordinary, rural people and how religious sensibilities mix with realities to cause us to think and act as we do. I have not been able to unravel all the intricacies involved in these matters, but I enjoy pondering them. Whether you call my life blessed, charmed, or just plain lucky, it has been a good one.

I have not been back to Reelfoot since writing this book; that is a mistake that needs to be rectified. Reviews of the book have generally been good, but I have no idea how people at the lake feel about the treatment I have given their story. Over the years, their friends and relatives have ensured that I not forget Reelfoot; by telephone and mail they have peppered me with new bits of information about the night riding incident and family members who participated in it. They want to know if I know more about the place and its people than I wrote in the book. The answer is no.

Indeed, there is a great deal more to be learned about the lake and the daily lives of the people who worked, prayed, and drank hard there in the early years of the twentieth century and who rose up to defend their rights, as they saw them, against the encroachments of outsiders who sought to displace them. Had I the intention of retelling the story, I would put much more emphasis on matters of social justice—on the tension between social and legal justice that is with us everywhere, all the time. When I did the research in the late 1950s, my social conscience was not as well honed as it is now, nor was my appreciation of legend, myth, the oral tradition, backwoods culture, and spiritual yearnings. The lore of Reelfoot Lake remains as powerful today as it was then, even if it is deeply lodged in the crevices of memory. The story and meaning of Reelfoot needs to be known and spread, for it carries historical lessons as well as moral and ethical teachings appropriate for today's world.

And I need to return to the lake for a thoughtful reunion with place and people.

BIBLIOGRAPHY

Primary Sources

INTERVIEWS BY AUTHOR

Jim Caksackkar, Joe Hogg, Joe Johnson, Fon Lasater, Harry McQueen, Bud Morris, and Fred Pinion, all of the Reelfoot Lake Region (Obion County) and self-admitted former Night Riders.

Ben Capell of Memphis, officer in state militia which served at Camp Nemo.

Cleve Donaldson of Tiptonville (Lake County), mayor of that city during the night riding era.

Tom J. Easterwood of Union City, sheriff of Obion County in night riding days.

John W. Hall of Tiptonville, Lake County constable in 1908–1909.

Mrs. G. W. Haynes of Memphis, widow of Judge Harris.

Mrs. T. B. Hooker of Memphis, daughter of Governor Malcolm R. Patterson.

Ben James of Memphis, state militiaman at Camp Nemo.

Mrs. L. D. Killion of Union City, niece of Attorney General D. J. Caldwell.

W. M. Miles of Union City, attorney who was a friend of J. C. Harris and who observed Night Rider legal proceedings.

Carlos Neely of Hornbeak, a Night Rider victim.

Seymour Osborne of Samburg, resident of Reelfoot district in 1908–1909.

Ham Patterson of Memphis, son of Governor Patterson.

Mrs. Guy Settle of Samburg, resident of lake region in 1908–1909.

Ange Shaw of Samburg, step-son of John Shaw, operator of Samburg fish docks in 1908.

Thomas Southworth of Union City, professional photographer in that city during Night Rider era.

Mrs. Truma Smith of Tiptonville, daughter of Squire George W. Wynne, a Night Rider victim.

Hillsman Taylor of Memphis, son of R. Z. Taylor, a victim of the Riders. H. Taylor also assisted in prosecution of the clansmen.

William Tidwell of Samburg, resident of lake district in 1908–1909.

Will Woodring of near Samburg, brother-in-law of David Walker, the Negro slain by the Riders.

DOCUMENTS

Patterson, Malcolm R. Papers. (in the Tennessee State Archives, Nashville).

Swiggart, W. H. Letter to Paul J. Vanderwood, 1956.

Tennessee. "North Carolina Land Grants, Charter Books A-1, 9, C." (in the Tennessee State Archives, Nashville).

Tennessee. *Public Acts.* 1903–1914.

Tennessee. Circuit Court. "Records of the Circuit Court, Minute Book J." (in the Obion County Courthouse, Union City, Tenn.).

Tennessee. "Records of the Circuit Court, Minute Book K." (in the Obion County Courthouse, Union City, Tenn.).

Tennessee. Department of Education. "Annual Reports of Obion County Superintendent to State Superintendent." Years ending June 30, 1892, 1893, and 1905. (in the Tennessee State Archives, Nashville).

Tennessee. 56th General Assembly, 1909. "H. R. 806: Bill to purchase easement to fish and hunt on Reelfoot Lake . . ." (manuscript in the Tennessee State Archives, Nashville).

Tennessee. 56th General Assembly, 1909. House. "House Joint Resolution No. 26—Relative to Reelfoot Lake." Adopted by the House on February 17, 1909. (manuscript in the Tennessee State Archives, Nashville).

Tennessee. 56th General Assembly, 1909. House. Reelfoot Lake Committee. "Report of the special committee appointed to investigate conditions at Reelfoot Lake," in *House Journal of the Fifty-Sixth General Assembly of the State of Tennessee.* Nashville, Tenn.: McQuiddy Printing Co., 1909, pp. 489–507.

Tennessee. Supreme Court. "Docket of the Supreme Court, Minute Book 44." (manuscript in the office of the Supreme Court Clerk, Tennessee State Courthouse, Jackson, Tenn.).

U. S. Bureau of Census. "Tenth Census (1880): Population," XXV (Tennessee: counties of Obion, Overton, and Perry). (manuscript in the Tennessee State Archives, Nashville).

————. *Twelfth Census of the United States Taken in the Year 1900.* Vol. 1, Population, Pt. 1. Washington, D. C.: United States Census Office, 1901.

————. *Thirteenth Census of the United States Taken in the Year 1910.* Vols. III, Population, and VII, Agriculture. Washington, D. C.: Government Printing Office, 1913.

Secondary Sources

BOOKS

Abernethy, Thomas P. *From Frontier to Plantation in Tennessee.* Memphis, Tenn.: Memphis State College Press, 1955.

Folmsbee, Stanley John, Corlew, Robert E., and Mitchell, Enoch L. *History of Tennessee.* New York: Lewis Historical Publishing Co., 1960.

Fuller, Myron L. *The New Madrid Earthquake.* (U. S. Geological Survey, Bulletin 494) Washington: Government Printing Office, 1912.

Gilchrist, Annie Sommers. *The Night-Rider's Daughter.* Nashville, Tenn.: Marshall & Bruce Co., 1910.

Goodspeed Publishing Company (ed.). *History of Tennessee.* Nashville: Goodspeed Publishing Co., 1887.

Hamer, Philip M. (ed.). *Tennessee, a History, 1632-1932.* 4 vols. New York: American Historical Society, Inc., 1933.

Lefler, Hugh Talmage, and Newsome, Albert Ray. *North Carolina: the History of a Southern State.* Chapel Hill: University of North Carolina Press, 1963.

Lowery, Woodbury. *The Spanish Settlements within the Present Limits of the United States, 1513-1561.* New York: G. P. Putnam's Sons, 1901.

Lyell, Charles. *A Second Visit to the United States of America.* 2 vols. New York: Harper & Bros., 1849.

Marshall, E. H. (ed.). *History of Obion County, Towns and Communities, Churches, Schools, Farming, Factories, Social and Political.* Union City, Tenn.: The Daily Messenger, 1941.

Nolte, Vincent. *Fifty Years in both Hemispheres or, Reminiscences of the Life of a Former Merchant.* New York: Redfield, 1854.

Old Times in West Tennessee. Memphis: W. G. Cheeney, 1873.

Purcell, Martha G. *Birth of Reelfoot Lake.* Paducah, Ky.: Paducah Printing Co., 1929.

Walker, Paul E. *Illustrated History of Reelfoot Lake.* [Ridgely, Tenn., 1929.]

Williams, Samuel Cole (ed.) *Adair's History of the American Indians.* Johnson City, Tenn.: Watauga Press, 1930.

_____. *Beginnings of West Tennessee in the Land of the Chickasaws, 1541-1841.* Johnson City: Watauga Press, 1930.

_____. *History of the Lost State of Franklin.* Johnson City: Watauga Press, 1924.

ARTICLES

"A Dramatic Trial of Night Riders," *Current Literature,* XLVI (February, 1909), 123-26.

Glenn, L. C. "The Geography and Geology of Reelfoot Lake," *Journal of the Tennessee Academy of Science,* VIII (January, 1933), 3-12.

Hall, Arthur Cleveland. "The Reelfoot Lake Night Riders," *The Independent,* LXVI (January 14, 1909), 78-84.

Humphreys, Cecil C. "The Formation of Reelfoot Lake and Consequent Land and Social Problems," *West Tennessee Historical Society Papers,* XIV (1960), 32-72.

"Lawlessness in the South," *The Outlook,* XC (October 31, 1908), 461–62.

Marquis, Don. "Menace of the Mask, pt. I: Tennessee's Tragic Story of Night Riders who Lynched at Reelfoot Lake," *Uncle Remus's, the Home Magazine,* XXIV (December, 1908), 15–21.

————. "Menace of the Mask, pt. IV: Sentencing of Night Riders at *Uncle Remus's, the Home Magazine,* XXIV (January, 1909), 9–10.

————. "Menace of the Mask, pt. IV: Sentencing of Night Riders at Union City. Personalities in the Reelfoot Region." *Uncle Remus's, the Home Magazine,* XXV (March, 1909), 20–21.

McGill, J. T., and Craig, W. W. "The Ownership of Reelfoot Lake," *Journal of the Tennessee Academy of Science,* VIII (January, 1933), 13–21.

Nelson, Wilbur A. "Reelfoot—An Earthquake Lake," *National Geographic Magazine,* XLV (January, 1924), 94–114.

"The Night Rider Folly," *The Independent,* LXV (October 8, 1908), 850–51.

"Reaping the Whirlwind," *The Nation,* LXXXVII (November 5, 1908), 428–29.

"Reelfoot Lake Night-Riders on Trial," *The Independent,* LXV (December 31, 1908), 1584–85.

Taylor, Hillsman. "The Night Riders of West Tennessee," *West Tennessee Historical Society Papers,* VI (1952), 72–86.

"Tennessee Murderers Condemned," *The Outlook,* XCI (January 16, 1909), 92.

UNPUBLISHED WORKS

Humphreys, Cecil C. "The History of the Reelfoot Lake Region." Unpublished Master's thesis, University of Tennessee, Knoxville, 1938.

Lowe, Walter Edgar. "History of Reelfoot Lake." Unpublished Master's thesis, George Peabody College for Teachers, Nashville, Tenn., 1930.

NEWSPAPERS

Atlanta Constitution. October 18, 1908–July 10, 1909.
Atlanta Journal. October 18, 1908–July 10, 1909.
Camden Chronicle. (Camden, Tenn.). 1908–1909.
Carroll County Democrat (Huntingdon, Tenn.). 1908–1909.
Chattanooga Daily Times. October, 1908–August, 1909.
Courier-Journal (Louisville). October, 1908–August, 1909.
Dresden Enterprise and Sharon Tribune (Dresden, Tenn.). 1908–1909.
Fayette Falcon (Somerville, Tenn.). 1908–1909.
Fayetteville Observer (Tenn.). 1908–1909.
Hardeman Free Press (Bolivar, Tenn.). 1908–1909.
Hickman Courier (Ky.). 1908–1909.
Lake County News (Tiptonville, Tenn.). 1908–1909.
Louisville Herald. October, 1908–August, 1909.
McNairy County Independent (Selmer, Tenn.). 1908–1909.
Milan Exchange (Milan, Tenn.). 1908–1909.
Nashville American. October, 1908–August, 1909.
Nashville Banner. October, 1908–August, 1909.
Nashville Tennessean. October, 1908–August, 1909.
New Orleans Times-Picayune. October 18, 1908–July 10, 1909.

News-Scimitar (Memphis, Tenn.). October, 1908–August, 1909, and January, 1914.

New York Herald. October 18, 1908–July 10, 1909.

New York Tribune. October 18, 1908–July 10, 1909.

St. Louis Globe-Democrat. October 18, 1908–July 10, 1909.

St. Louis Post-Dispatch. October 18, 1908–July 10, 1909.

South Pittsburg Hustler (Marion County, Tenn.). 1908–1909.

The Commercial Appeal (Memphis, Tenn.). October, 1908–August, 1909.

The New York Times. October 18, 1908–July 10, 1909.

The States-Graphic (Brownsville, Tenn.). January–December, 1908.

The Sun (New York City). October 18, 1908–July 10, 1909.

The World (New York City). October 18, 1908–July 10, 1909.

Trenton Herald-Democrat (Tenn.). 1908–1909.

Weakley County Press (Martin, Tenn.). 1908–1909.

INDEX

159